HOW TO GENERATE WORD OF MOUTH ADVERTISING

HOW TO GENERATE WORD OF MOUTH ADVERTISING

---

101 Easy and Inexpensive Ways to Promote Your Business

Godfrey Harris
with
Gregrey J Harris

1995

First US Edition

1st Printing—October 1995
2nd Printing—April 1996

The Americas Group
9200 Sunset Blvd., Suite 404
Los Angeles, California 90069
U.S.A.

ISBN:
0-935047-19-0

Library of Congress Catalog Card Number:
95-33996

Library of Congress Cataloging-in-Publication Data

3 2280 00518 5418

Harris, Godfrey, 1937-
    How to generate word of mouth advertising : 101 easy and
inexpensive ways to promote your business / Godfrey Harris, with
Gregrey J. Harris. -- 1st US ed.
    p.   cm.
    Includes index.
    ISBN 0-935047-19-0
    1. Marketing.   2. Word-of-mouth advertising.   3. Consumer
satisfaction.   I. Harris, Gregrey J., 1962-   . II. Title.
HF5415.122.H367   1995
658.8'2--dc20   95-33996
                                                                  CIP

Printed in the United States of America
Complete Reproduction Service, Inc.
Book Design
Godfrey Harris

The idea that
word of mouth advertising
could be successfully generated
and need not be left to luck was first
suggested in our book,
Talk Is Cheap.

While we provided dozens
of ways to create positive
word of mouth advertising—
and prevent negative comments—
we subsequently developed
many more ideas that
could be immediately adapted to
almost any business.

In this book we offer
step-by-step *recipes*
to take ideas from the printed page
to a customer's lips.

GH
GJH

ALSO BY GODFREY HARRIS WITH GREGREY J HARRIS

Power Buying
Talk Is Cheap

ALSO BY GODFREY HARRIS

European Union Handbook and Business Titles (with Adelheid Hasenknopf)
The Panamanian Problem (with Guillermo de St. Malo A.)
Mapping Russia and Its Neighbors (with Sergei A. Diakonov)
The Fascination of Ivory
Invasion (with David S. Behar)
The Ultimate Black Book
The Panamanian Perspective
Promoting International Tourism (with Kenneth M. Katz)
Commercial Translations (with Charles Sonabend)
From Trash to Treasure (with Barbara DeKovner-Mayer)
Panama's Position
The Quest for Foreign Affairs Officers (with Francis Fielder)
The History of Sandy Hook, New Jersey
Outline of Social Sciences
Outline of Western Civilization

TABLE OF CONTENTS

EMPOWER YOUR CUSTOMERS 63

PROVIDE INFORMATION AND THEY'LL SEND OTHERS 87

INTRODUCTION

How many times have you heard that the best kind of advertising comes from "word of mouth?" It's true. Most of us have become nearly immune to the hundreds of commercials seeking to capture our attention every day: We fast-forward the VCR, punch another button on the car radio, flip past the ad pages in a magazine, or try to glance beyond the billboards on the road. But when a friend recommends a product or business, we not only pay attention, we are more likely to act on the recommendation.

Many believe that favorable word of mouth comments come from plain luck. While we would certainly agree that good fortune plays a role in most business successes, this book offers 101 ways to help stack the odds in your favor.

Marketing is Easy!

The ways are presented as recipes, complete with the key ingredients you will need to make them work for you. Like many foods you enjoy and then learn to prepare, many of the ideas are deceptively simple to implement. In fact, we are amazed that more businesses don't specifically try to develop word of mouth marketing *strategies*, given its low cost and high success rate.

Most businesses are built on good ideas, services and products, yet many fail because they lack strong marketing. A good marketing plan doesn't require a big budget; it doesn't require an MBA or a lot of experience, either. It does demand some creative thinking and some common sense. We'll try to spark your creative juices in the pages that follow, but you will have to rely on your business and customer knowledge to apply the ideas to your own particular situation.

Everyone Has the Talent

We recently conducted a research study for a high technology firm. We asked the firm's customers how they got *their* customers. The answers were quite surprising. Almost half said that they came primarily through word of mouth advertising. Upon detailed study of the survey responses, however, it became clear that these businesses were doing nothing to generate positive word of mouth comments.

Word of mouth referrals can be stimulated. How many people have moved to a new neighborhood and asked someone for a good Chinese restaurant? How many businesses buy a new software program for their computers after hearing it extolled by someone else? While the first example relies on an interested buyer initiating a conversation, the second suggests that businesses ought to find ways to encourage customers into having conversations with potential buyers.

The Word of Mouth Formula

Here's everything you need to know about marketing in three basic lessons.

Lesson One: **People buy products or services because the *cost* is less than the *value* that they receive from the product or service.**

Cost: Don't assume that everyone sees the price tag on an item as its cost. Think of the cost of a music CD to a teenager working at a fast food restaurant compared to a successful business person. Both pay the same price, but the cost to the teenager is substantially higher because the teenager's earnings are much lower. There are also intangible costs. For example, the teenager may have to ride for a half-hour on a bus to get to the store, while the businessman views it as a short drive.

Value: Value is a personal thing. What one person values in a product may not be the same as another person. Someone exhausted on a blazing hot day may view a $3 glass of lemonade as providing $20 worth of value. On a cold, snowy day, that same lemonade may have no value at all to anyone.

Lesson Two: **Exceed customers' expectations.**

Expectations: The product we sell and the price we charge may mean little if the customer expects a lot more. Everyone expects to pay a certain price, receive a certain value, and be provided with a particular bundle of services. Comments are generated when these expectations are substantially exceeded. The key is not only to know what customers expect of you, but to figure out how to provide even more.

Lesson Three: **Be very clear with your customers what you want them to do.**

Ask for what you want. Customers can be quite cooperative and can easily be motivated to talk about your business to their friends (assuming you've successfully mastered Lessons One and Two). Successful word of mouth marketers will develop ways to give their customers a gentle nudge to get them going.

There's A Catch

Sure, word of mouth advertising is easy, but this isn't something that you do once and forget. You will constantly need to evaluate your customer's expectations; they will change over time. Further, your competition, if they are half as good as you, will be adjusting their product offering, pricing, and service to meet your new standard. The hurdle turns into a high jump and eventually a pole vault. The bar, which represents the standard of excellence you must deliver, is continuously being raised by the marketplace—if not by your competitors, then by your customers expecting greater benefits.

But don't worry. The good news is that while marketing is easy, there are few people who do it, let alone do it well. Focus on understanding why your customers come to you and how you can continue to delight them. Secondly, focus on techniques you can use to get them to be a partner in your business and help refer more customers to you.

Let's Go!

That's it. You're now an expert. Just one other point to remember. Adam Smith wrote: "It is not from the benevolence of the butcher, the brewer, or the baker that we expect our dinner, but from their regard to their own self interest." Smith reasoned that If the baker laces his bread with sawdust, the customers will know, the customers will tell their friends, and all of them will stop buying the baker's bread—word of mouth at the very root of the theory underlying capitalism. Smith's ideas are as valid today as they were in the 18th century.

CATEGORIES OF GENERATING WORD OF MOUTH ADVERTISING

We have divided the 101 recipes for generating word of mouth advertising into the categories below. Businesses should consider implementing one program at a time to test their effectiveness with their customers, then decide whether implementing several in different categories simultaneously or many different programs over a period of time is better.

Give Something Away

Those who receive gifts tend to display them and talk about those who provide them.

Do It Differently

Any unusual activity or process that benefits a customer tends to evoke favorable comments about the sponsor of that activity or process.

Empower Your Customers

Provide those who buy from you with awards and privileges to share with others—a great way to make new friends for your business.

Provide Information

Give your customers new, important, or humorous information to share with others and benefit from the ensuring discussions arising from the inevitable: "Where'd you hear that?"

Pay Attention to Reactions

How people deal with each and every aspect of your business yields important clues about what they will say about your business and products to others.

Minimize Negative Comments

No business can fully avoid negative comments—whether deserved or not—but all businesses can minimize the potential damage through attentive responses to the problems exposed.

Get It Right

Not only can word of mouth advertising be stimulated, it can be sharpened and directed to produce the results desired.

GIVE SOMETHING AWAY

Those who receive gifts tend to display them as well as talk about those who provide them.

AWARD A SURPRISE REBATE

After completing a job, return a small sum of money to your customers to share "savings."

Three weeks after receiving a final payment, send the customer a small check with a note explaining that you realized a rebate from one of your suppliers and that you like to share savings with your customers. Here is an example of the letter you might write:

Do you think an un-expected windfall as described in this letter might cause some comment from the recipient to friends and relatives?

```
Date                        ABC Repairs
                            Street Address
                            City, State ZIP

Dear Customer:
        We hope you are pleased
with the job we recently com-
pleted for you.
        We have just learned that
our supplier has awarded us a
volume discount for the business
we give him. As is our practice,
we like to share the savings we
realize with our customers.
Please find enclosed a refund
check for $19.75.
        We look forward to working
with you or your colleagues in
the future.
                Sincerely,

                Alan B. Cole
                Owner
```

USE THIS WORD OF MOUTH GENERATOR FOR LARGE JOBS ONLY AND MAKE THE REBATE AN ODD AMOUNT. FOR EXAMPLE, GIVE $19.75 ON AN INVOICE IN THE $500 RANGE. IT ISN'T THE AMOUNT THAT CAUSES CONVERSATION, IT IS THE UNEXPECTED NATURE OF THE GIFT BEING AWARDED THAT DOES.

THIS IS A PARTICULARLY EFFECTIVE WAY TO GET CUSTOMERS TO TALK ABOUT TAILORS, UPHOLSTERERS, PRINTERS, MOVERS, REPAIR SPECIALISTS IN ALL FIELDS, AND OTHER CUSTOM CRAFTS PEOPLE.

SEND A PRESENT

*Pick an obscure point on the annual calendar—
Arbor Day, the Anniversary of the Queen's
Accession to the Throne, the Autumnal Equinox—
as the day to send a gift or card.*

Once you have selected a day to commemorate each year, choose a small gift or unique greeting card that will remind your customers and clients of your business or product and tell them the reason that you are thinking about them on the particular day chosen. Here is an example of a message that might be sent:

> ABC Clothes
> Street Address
> City, State ZIP
>
> Dear Customer:
>   As always, Flag Day heralds the good things that summer brings. This June 14th, we are again going to display our range of shorts and shirts. Please come to our store with a friend to receive a 40% discount on any purchase made.
>   Sincerely,
>
>   Alex Benjamin Cox

Instead of sending a card, choose a gift with your logo. Advertising specialty firms can help you select an appropriate gift that carries just the right message.

F YOU ADOPT THIS IDEA, BE CONSISTENT FROM YEAR TO YEAR. WHILE YOU MAY NOT GENERATE A NOTICEABLE REACTION THE FIRST TIME YOU USE IT, BY THE SECOND OR THIRD YEAR IT WILL BECOME A CONVERSATION TOPIC AMONG YOUR CUSTOMERS AND CLIENTS.

THIS IS A PARTICULARLY GOOD WAY FOR ANY BUSINESS THAT PRIDES ITSELF ON ORIGINALITY AND ENJOYS THE HUMOROUS SIDE OF COMMERCE—ADVERTISING AGENCIES, ARTISTS, CONSULTANTS, DESIGNERS, ETC.

PACKAGE A TWO-FER

*Two-fers are products presented in pairs—
one item in the pair for the customer to use,
the other to be "given" away.*

Most word of mouth promotion relies on the customer being able to *describe to someone else* what he or she liked about a product or service. This word of mouth concept is much more direct—the customer is provided with an actual example of your goods to give to someone else to try.

Because this technique is designed to create a chain marketing reaction, all two-fer items should also be packaged with a coupon, discount order blank, or other device to permit those in the chain to obtain an additional example to give to someone else.

The possibilities of two-fer packages seem infinite. We present just two below as Recipes No. 4 and 5.

A TWO-FER FOR GROCERY COMPANIES AND PHARMACIES

Put *two* examples of any new item you want customers to try—a jar of mustard, a natural cereal, some tropical fruit juice, a metal polish, hair spray, cough drops, or the like—into an identifiable plastic bag or other packaging with two copies of a flyer that describes how the item can best be enjoyed and suggesting that the second item be given to a relative, friend, or colleague.

ATTACH TWO DISCOUNT COUPONS AT THE BOTTOM OF EACH FLYER—ONE FOR THE ORIGINAL RECIPIENT OF THE TWO-FER TO USE, AND THE OTHER FOR THE RELATIVE, FRIEND OR COLLEAGUE TO GIVE TO SOMEONE ELSE ONCE HE OR SHE HAS TRIED THE PRODUCT.

A TWO-FER FOR PUBLISHERS

Put a paper wrapper around two copies of a book, tape, journal, CD-ROM, 3.5" disk, or other published work. Print the following note on the wrapper:

> We are certain that once you have read this book [heard this tape, etc.] you will want to refer to it in the future. It's also probable that you will want to share the insights with someone else. As a result, we have enclosed a second copy of our book [tape, etc.] for you to give to a relative, friend, or colleague.

While the concept of selling two books or tapes for the price of one may seem to add cost to a product, remember that the added volume being manufactured can reduce the unit price of each item to a manageable amount and create impressive distribution figures that make an important statement in themselves.

THIS CONCEPT WORKS PARTICULARLY WELL WITH SELF-HELP AND HOW TO TITLES—BOOKS, TAPES, AND OTHER MATERIAL THAT PEOPLE WILL WANT TO RETAIN FOR THEIR OWN FUTURE REFERENCE, BUT MAY ALSO WANT TO SHARE WITH OTHERS. PUBLISHERS OF PHILOSOPHY, POETRY, AND REFERENCE BOOKS WILL FIND THIS A GOOD WAY TO BUILD SALES.

PROVIDE A RELATED SERVICE

Find a natural linkage between your business and the service or product you can offer to generate the conversations you need.

Would you recommend an insurance agent if he or she arranged to have your fire extinguishers checked and recharged at no cost to you? If you were a real estate agent, do you think people would talk about you if you offered to have their house numbers regularly painted on the curb in front of their house or on their trash bins? If you sold telephone equipment or other communication devices, do you think providing a service to clean and disinfect that equipment periodically for customers might provoke comment to others that would be of benefit to your sales goals?

THE KEY TO MAKING THIS CONCEPT WORK AS A WORD OF MOUTH GENERATOR IS IS NOT SO MUCH THE VALUE OF THE PRODUCT OR SERVICE INVOLVED; IT IS THE OCCASIONAL AND RANDOM NATURE OF WHAT IS GIVEN AWAY AS WELL AS ITS PERCEIVED USEFULNESS.

THE POWER OF PHONE CARDS

Telephone cards are a mechanism that permits the prepayment of long distance phone calls.

Phone cards encourage the use of the telephone and the telephone is clearly one of the primary ways to communicate word of mouth comments.

As such, adopting these cards as a promotional tool can become an important way to promote favorable word of mouth comments about a product or service.

Two specific Recipes involving the use of phone cards can be found on the pages that follow

ONCE A TELEPHONE CARD SPONSOR HAS PAID FOR AN INITIAL VALUE OF CALLS—AND THAT VALUE HAS BEEN CONSUMED BY THE RECIPIENT—THE USER CAN REFILL THE CARD FOR ADDITIONAL TELEPHONE USAGE TIME BY MERELY USING HIS OR HER OWN CREDIT CARD.

A PHONE CARD FOR TRAVELERS

*Phone cards can promote a business and
provide an incentive to talk at the same time.*

The two cards above were developed to give to people travelling to the United States from Great Britain. They serve as a reward for choosing a certain airline or booking the trip through a particular travel agency. But they also serve as a mechanism for the caller to phone home to discuss his or her travel while *experiencing* it.

Nothing could be more effective in the field of word of mouth promotions than having people talk to others about a place or event in the middle of enjoying that place or event. The folks back home get news and impressions while they are fresh.

The telephone card helps convey those feelings in a way that few other word of mouth tools can.

A PHONE CARD CARRIER

Phone cards can be presented to customers attached to a folder that includes a promotional message from the sponsor.

We believe the sponsor of a phone card should include some encouragement to recipients to talk about their experience with its services or products to friends, relatives, and colleagues. Here is an example of a word of mouth promotional message we wrote for the potential use of a client.

A Message from the Los Angeles County Music & Performing Arts Commission

To Old and New Friends:

We hope that you are enjoying your current stay in the Los Angeles area and that you have had an opportunity to see some of the places that give this city and its surrounding communities their unique reputation. Like people everywhere, we are always curious about the places and events that make the biggest impression on our visitors—the moments that you will remember most vividly and that you will want to describe to your friends and family when you return home.

If you have just arrived in the area or still have some time left, may we suggest a few

Word of Mouth
Pitch No. 1

23

sites and some places that we think you shouldn't miss. Most of these you will have seen on television or in the movies; but in person they make an even more lasting memory: The Hollywood Bowl, the Los Angeles Music Center, the Greek Theatre, the Los Angeles County Museum of Art, the Getty Museum, the Griffith Park Observatory, the Los Angeles Zoo, and so on. We also have a host of spectacular new facilities that you may not know much about—the Museum of Contemporary Art, the Fowler at UCLA, the Petersen Automotive Museum, the Museum of Tolerance, the Craft and Folk Art Museum, and much more. They are all worth your time.

Word of Mouth Pitch No. 2

We hope you put your Personal LA Telecom Calling Card to good use and that you will take time to tell your friends and family what they should be sure to see and do during *their* visit to Los Angeles in the years to come. And if you care to let us know some of your thoughts about Los Angeles, that would be very interesting for us as well.

Word of Mouth Pitch No. 3

Executive Director

NOTE THE MESSAGE ENCOURAGED THE RECIPIENTS OF THE CARD TO THINK A LITTLE ABOUT WHAT THEY WANT TO TELL THEIR LISTENERS BEFORE EXPLAINING WHAT THEY HAVE DONE AND SEEN. BY GETTING SOMEONE TO THINK ABOUT HOW TO DESCRIBE A PLACE OR EVENT, THE SPEAKER BECOMES MORE ARTICULATE AND A BETTER ADVERTISING VEHICLE FOR THE SPONSOR.

RECYCLE WRAP

*Create a generic gift wrap bag, box,
and/or ribbon that invites recyling.*

Many wise shoppers save the gift boxes and ribbons from fine stores to use in wrapping their own gifts for others—whether or not the new item came from that particular establishment. It is a nice idea that can be turned into a word of mouth generator.

Adopt a gift box design, ribbon, and/or pattern—or wrapping paper and no-harm self-sticking tape—that *encourages* recycling. Be sure to identify the provider of the recycled gift wrapping. Put a card in with the gift—or create a rubber stamp for use on the bottom of the box or the back of the paper and ribbon—explaining the recycling concept. Here is an example of such a message:

> This generic gift wrap is made from recycled products and has been provided by "Your Favorite Department Store" in the hope that the recipient of the gift will save this wrapping for later use when giving a gift to someone else.

THIS WORD OF MOUTH CONCEPT IS DESIGNED FOR USE BY SUCH RETAIL ESTABLISHMENTS AS CLOTHING STORES, BEAUTY SUPPLY SHOPS, ANTIQUE DEALERS, GIFT STORES, AND THE LIKE.

CREATE A UNIQUE SOUVENIR

*Find something that you can give away
that others will want to display long
enough to start a conversation.*

The souvenir item might be something to wear—an unusual piece of clothing or an accessory—or something to hang on a wall—a piece of artwork or a particularly impressive certificate. Whatever the item, it should be designed to catch an eye and provoke a question to generate conversations about the provider.

Souvenir items are best if they are inexpensive enough to give away; if they have to be sold, it should be done at cost. Today, many businesses sell caps, T-shirts, and other items imprinted with their logos, slogans, or other identifying elements and even treat these products as separate profit centers—Porche, Marlboro, and *Phantom of the Opera* come to mind. While these products certainly can provoke conversation, their reach may be limited because their cost prohibits wide distribution.

In our view, it is better to give something away for free than to try to open a new profit center; the business generated from word of mouth comments may, in fact, surpass the money earned on the sale of a few products not generally germane to a core business.

GIVE AWAY A *SPECIAL* HAT

Hats are fun, useful, and particularly effective as billboards to generate conversations.

The owners of many businesses do conventional baseball-style caps with their names and/or logos embossed on the front—hats with Caterpillar and NBC seem everywhere. They are nice, but by now pretty ordinary.

Businesses that really want attention should do their give aways differently to provoke notice and conversation—particularly if they are part of the tourist trade. For example:

- American attractions and restaurants might give away a replica 10-gallon cowboy hat;
- English attractions and restaurants might do a form of the bowler hat;
- French boutiques or cafes might create a beret that can be identified with their establishment.

Whatever the design, make sure the hat brim, band, or ribbon carries the establishment's name with an inside label to provide an easy reference for location and telephone number.

Of course, hats may be too blatant or too bulky for some foreign visitors to accept—even as gifts for others. In that case, we suggest a little booklet providing the background on a product or the history of a facility—well illustrated and richly detailed—to lay yet another foundation for conversations with friends and relatives back home.

TO BE (PROPRIETARY ITEMS) OR NOT TO BE

Items that are identified with the provider are always particularly effective.

Offering a product as your own house brand is always impressive— whether silver polish or shoe polish. Even if the ingredients or design for this product are not original with your firm, the impact will nevertheless be significant.

Look in the *Thomas Catalog* at a library or a Business-to-Business telephone directory to determine who might manufacture the item you want to label as your own. Check with the owner of the brand name itself to find out if they package the product for others. Nearly all well-known product types can be duplicated, packaged, and labeled as your proprietary product, just as many supermarkets and stores buy from generic manufacturers to sell products as house brands. For example:

> *Tubes of sunscreen can be given away to clients and customers and labeled as their own product by golf pros, tennis instructors, barbecue suppliers, gardening stores, or any other firm involved in outdoor services and products.*

If the item seems to have been packaged exclusively for the provider, it becomes an effective basis for stimulating conversations when it is used, when extra tubes are given away by customers, or when the total value of a competitors' products or services are compared.

BOTTLE YOUR SALAD DRESSING—
OR ANYTHING ELSE

Take the aspect of your business that makes it unique among all of your competitors and find a way to "package" it.

Every delicatessen, snack bar, sandwich shop, restaurant, and catering business makes something that defines its style in cooking or food preparation. Find a way to "bottle" and label samples of that one item so that customers can share it with their friends, relatives, and associates.

The publisher of this book produces miniature versions of the books it sells. A little four- or eight-page sample has proven to be a terrific give-away to provide just enough information to intrigue the recipient into wanting to acquire the real thing.

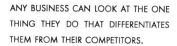

ANY BUSINESS CAN LOOK AT THE ONE THING THEY DO THAT DIFFERENTIATES THEM FROM THEIR COMPETITORS.

ONCE ISOLATED, THEY CAN CREATE A TECHNIQUE THAT PERMITS ITS DISTRIBUTION IN A MINIATURE OR SAMPLE FORM.

FAIRY MESSAGES®
FOR EVERY CUSTOMER

Fairy Messages® are statements that convey something positive about another person, such as: "You are the spark that becomes a dancing flame;" and "You are the warm wind whispering secrets."

The words are found on colorful little oval cards that are a delight to give or leave for someone as a surprise; they are instant smile makers. They are also a wonderful way to make a business card more meaningful and convey an important message at the same time to others. Here is a sample of a thank you card we recommended to an organization we work with:

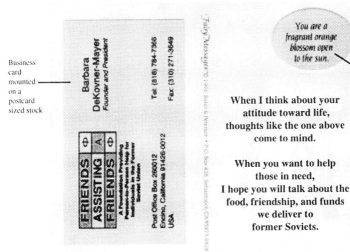

Business card mounted on a postcard sized stock

Barbara DeKovner-Mayer
Founder and President

Tel: (818) 784-7366
Fax: (310) 271-3649

FRIENDS ASSISTING FRIENDS

Post Office Box 260012
Encino, California 91426-0012
USA

You are a fragrant orange blossom open to the sun.

Actual Fairy Message® mounted on the card

When I think about your attitude toward life, thoughts like the one above come to mind.

When you want to help those in need, I hope you will talk about the food, friendship, and funds we deliver to former Soviets.

FAIRY MESSAGES® ALWAYS SEEM TO PROVOKE SMILES FROM THE RECIPIENT AND A LOT OF INTEREST AMONG THE RECIPIENT'S COMPANIONS. IF YOU WOULD LIKE TO DISCUSS A WORD OF MOUTH PROGRAM INVOLVING FAIRY MESSAGES®, WRITE TO

THE CREATORS OF THESE NOVEL MESSAGES:

Baker & Peterson
PO Box 428
Sebastopol, California 95473 USA
Fx + (1) 707 829 2127

DO IT DIFFERENTLY

Any unusual activity or process that benefits a customer tends to evoke favorable comments about the sponsor of that activity or process.

THE DOUBLE POSTCARD

Postcards start conversations and generate positive word of mouth comments between the sender and the recipient.

To do a postcard a little differently from your competitors, try creating a *double* postcard. As the sample below demonstrates, the double postcard offers a large version to send to a friend, relative, or colleague through the mail and a smaller, identical version to keep as a souvenir to share personally with others when you return home.

THE EXCALIBUR HOTEL IN LAS VEGAS IS CALLED THE WORLD'S LARGEST HOTEL/ RESORT WITH MORE THAN 4,000 ROOMS AND A 50,000M^2 ENTERTAINMENT AREA. BECAUSE THE HOTEL IS OBVIOUSLY SOMETHING WORTH TALKING ABOUT, THE CARDS MAKE AN INEXPENSIVE WAY TO GET VISITORS TO TALK ABOUT THEIR EXPERIENCE IN THE FACILITY. BUS COMPANIES, HOSTELS, AND OTHER TOURIST TRADE FIRMS SHOULD CONSIDER THIS IDEA.

17

IF NOT MATCHBOOKS, THEN TRY SCRATCHBOOKS

Instead of a matchbook as a traditional reminder of a restaurant, hotel, or celebratory event, offer look-alike "books" containing scratch paper for notes.

As cigarette smoking continues to fall from favor in many areas of the world, matchbooks become anachronisms of a bygone era and of sustained interest only to collectors. But the idea of a free, useful gift to remind someone of where he or she has been and as a conversation starter, matchbooks remain very attractive.

As a result, we urge you to consider printing "scratchbooks" instead of matchbooks.

IF SCRATCH PAPER IS NOT SUITABLE TO BIND BETWEEN THE COVERS OF A "MATCHBOOK," ASK A TRADITIONAL MATCHBOOK PRINTER TO STAPLE IN A PEPPERMINT OR EVEN SEVERAL DISCOUNT COUPONS FOR A PRODUCT, SERVICE OR SPECIAL SOUVENIR FROM AN ESTABLISHMENT.

THE IDEA WORKS FOR RESTAURANTS, BARS, HOTELS, MOTELS, EVENT PLANNERS, AND ANY SERVICE BUSINESS SUCH AS ACCOUNTANTS, ENGINEERS, LAWYERS, CONSULTANTS, AND INSURANCE AGENTS TO PLACE IN THEIR RECEPTION AREAS.

A MIDDLE EASTERN CHRISTMAS CARD

*Nearly everyone seems to send
seasonal cards at Christmas time,
but how many stand out enough to evoke a comment?*

Last year we received a Christmas card that opened backwards—with the fold on the *right* side and the message on the inside *left hand* page.

As soon as we received this card from a client—it reminded us more of an Arabic brochure than a Christmas card—we called the sender to note the different look he had provided. He said that it had caused so much comment that he wished he had done it intentionally. He admitted that the printer had simply made a dumb mistake in reviewing the layout of the card's cover and message on the computer. By the time the error was discovered, it was too late in the holiday season to buy new stock and start afresh, so our client held his breath and sent the cards out anyway. In the end, they probably did him more good than a conventional holiday greeting.

BECAUSE PRINTING IS NOT THE BUSINESS OF THE COMPANY THAT SENT THIS CARD TO ITS CLIENTS, RECIPIENTS COULD BE AMUSED AT THE ERROR WITHOUT ANY CONNOTATION OF INEPTITUDE ATTACHING TO THE SENDER. TRY THIS IDEA IN OTHER MAILINGS YOU DO—PRINTING ENVELOPES UPSIDE DOWN OR USING COLORS WHERE WHITE IS NORMALLY EXPECTED. DIFFERENCES MAKE SOMETHING REMARKABLE—ONE OF THE KEYS TO GENERATING WORD OF MOUTH COMMENTS.

SEND "TASTERS" HOME

*As more and more people leave restaurants
with leftovers to take home, so it makes sense
to send samples along to share with others.*

Restaurants should pick a specialty item from their menu that has a long shelf life and requires little or no fussing to serve—a particular appetizer, spread, sauce, or dessert. Package the item in a sufficient quantity so that four can enjoy it; print a self-stick label on a computer-driver laser printer to identify the restaurant, and provide how-to-serve instructions. Present the item to patrons when they leave.

Be sure to have a few varieties available to be able to offer something different for each visit of repeat customers.

RESTAURANTS, CATERERS, DELICATESSENS, GOURMET SHOPS, ICE CREAM PARLORS, SANDWICH BARS, COFFEE HOUSES, TEA ROOMS, BAKERIES, EVEN HEALTH FOOD STORES AND FOOD MARKETS CAN USE THIS IDEA WITH CUSTOMERS WHO ARE NOT TAKING LEFTOVERS HOME. CREATE SOME OTHER CRITERIA—SPENDING ABOVE A CERTAIN AMOUNT OR FOR THOSE WHO ALSO ORDER SOMETHING EXTRA (WINE, PROPRIETARY PRODUCTS, SPECIALTIES, TOPPINGS, ETC.)—AS A WAY OF MAKING THE PRESENTATION SPECIAL.

SEND "TASTERS" HOME— BUT *WITH* A GIFT CERTIFICATE

For even greater impact, present a gift certificate to special customers along with a "taster."

The gift certificate suggested below is to give to the person with whom the "taster" is shared or to someone else.

CYBER CERTIFICATES

Any business can offer coupons for their customers to award to the customer's colleagues, clients, and contacts. We specially designed the certificate below for a New York research firm that conducts its business almost entirely over the Internet.

THE WORD OF MOUTH PRODUCT DESIGNED FOR METROQUEST CONSISTED OF THREE ELEMENTS: A COVER LETTER EXPLAINING THEIR PROGRAM; A CERTIFICATE FOR THE METROQUEST CUSTOMER TO AWARD; AND AN ACTION-FORCING CONFIRMATION MESSAGE, THAT ALSO SERVES AS A SECURITY MEASURE, FOR THE CLIENT TO TRANSMIT BACK TO METROQUEST.

THE MESSAGE FROM METROQUEST

Dear Client:

We hope that the research material MetroQuest recently provided has proven helpful. Like many businesses everywhere, the favorable impressions we make on our clients serve as an important testimonial to our skills and responsibility.

We trust that whatever you think we did well—the scope of our research, the speed of our response, the reasonableness of our fees, the extent of our search, or some other service we provided—might merit a favorable recommenda-

Put the words in their mouths.

tion to a colleague, customer, or contact. If so, we hope you will be good enough to award a Cyber Certificate in support of our efforts to continue to grow and improve our capabilities. The actual Certificate is on the way to you by mail; a replica is below.

Once you have decided who should receive this Certificate, please let us know the name of the individual receiving it on the accompanying MetroQuest Response Form (a copy of which is also below) so that we can respond promptly to their first search request.

In appreciation for your assistance and support with this program, we will be happy to give you a 10% discount from our standard pricing schedule for your continuing research needs within the succeeding 12 months.

Paul H. Smith
MetroQuest

METROQUEST RESPONSE FORM

To: MetroQuest   Date [   ]

Cyber Certificate 1515-95 02 101 has been awarded today to:

_____

PLEASE ENTER NAME OF RECIPIENT

CYBER CERTIFICATE

[THE NAME OF METROQUEST'S CLIENT IS INSERTED HERE]

is pleased to commend MetroQuest's research services to

ENTER THE NAME OF THE INDIVIDUAL TO WHOM THIS CERTIFICATE IS
FORWARDED

who may request a free search for information or specific data within 12 months of

ENTER THE DATE THIS CERTIFICATE IS AWARDED

Please contact MetroQuest directly to initiate your search—a value of $25.

Certificate Number

1515-95 02 101

Internet   MetroQuest@aol.com
☎   (1) 212 980 5660
fx   (1) 212 980 5660

MetroQuest Research Services
301 East 53rd Street—#1A
New York City, NY 10022 USA

MIXING APPLES & ORANGES—
LITERALLY

*As a health-conscious world learns
more about their diets, profit-conscious businesses
should learn more about what makes people talk.*

Candies have long been seen on counter tops and desk tops, dining tables and coffee tables. They appear not only at Halloween, but throughout the year as well. Smart marketers can use the concept, but do it differently and do it better. Instead of sweets, put out fresh fruit—tangerines, apples, bananas, grapes, plums, oranges, nectarines—or dried fruit—raisins, dates, prunes, apricots—for clients and customers to enjoy.

Those who use this concept should leave a card near the fruit bowl explaining the approach with words such as:

> *We hope you enjoy one of our healthy snacks during your visit to our offices and will mention to your friends the fresh ways we like to treat your needs.*

While the words may be a bit corny, they do tend to stick in the mind. A picture of a bowl of fruit on some of the firm's promotional material will reinforce the theme. If the client had not spoken about the unusual treat available in the office to others, the reminder should spark a conversation or at least a return visit.

ANY PROFESSIONAL OFFICE—CONSULTANTS, REAL ESATE BROKERS, ENGINEERS, LAWYERS, DOCTORS—AND ANY SERVICE BUSINESS—DRY CLEANERS, FURRIERS, PRINTERS, LOCKSMITHS, JEWELERS, ETC.— COULD BENEFIT FROM THIS IDEA.

MAKE YOUR PRODUCT FAMOUS

*Because personalities draw public attention,
provide a favorite individual with a sample of your product
in the hope that it might be given exposure
that engenders comments from others.*

Not all word of mouth advertising need originate from one person's direct experience to another. It is possible to generate effective word of mouth comments by getting people to remark on where they have seen a product in use or who else may be benefiting from it. For example, we once worked hard to develop a way to present a book to Russian President Boris N. Yeltsin during a state visit to Norway in order to get either a picture or a reaction that could be used in a marketing campaign.

Remember, also, that there are product placement brokers located in Hollywood, New York, Chicago, and elsewhere who negotiate the use of products in films, television, noncompetitive ads, shows, and theatrical productions. Note that the idea here is not to decorate a celebrity like a race car driver's coveralls, a golfer's visor, or a tennis player's sleeves, but merely to try to find a way to publicly link a personality or event to a product or service in a way that people will talk about.

WE RESERVE THIS CONCEPT FOR OUR WEALTHIER CLIENTS WHO ARE INVOLVED IN MANUFACTURIING, DISTRIBUTION, IMPORTING, AND OTHER AREAS WHERE THE CLIENT HAS DIRECT RESPONSIBILITY FOR THE PRODUCT AND ITS MARKETING. AS SUCH, THEY CAN CONTROL THE APPROACHES TO PRODUCERS, PERSONALITIES, AND BROKERS.

GET YOUR MESSAGE ON A CLOCK FACE

They can remind customers that its time to set an appointment.

Every service business performs routine activities for its clientele on a regular basis—accountants keep books, barbers cut hair, lawyers review wills, mechanics lubricate cars. Many companies will put their name or logo on a wristwatch and give the watch to *employees;* but very few think of putting a *message* and *telephone number* on an entire clock face—and giving it to a client to display on a desk, side table, wall, or in a reception area.

It can add a new dimension to an old idea. The message not only will bring your own clients back on a regular basis, but can spark questions from your client's clients about the clock's message. Here's a clock a barber could give to one of his lawyer patrons:

GETTING A STRONG, INTERESTING MESSAGE ON A CLOCK FACE IS NOT AS EASY AS IT SOUNDS. BUT ONCE PRODUCED SHOULD IN TURN PRODUCE RESULTS.

BUSINESSES AFFILIATED IN A LEAGUE (SEE RECIPE NO. 69) MIGHT PUT ALL THE MEMBERS' NAMES ON A CLOCK.

IT'S TIME FOR...

Remind clients of the need for a special service and encourage them to bring in a contact at the same time.

Beyond the routine services performed by professional firms are those specialized or exotic services that tend to differentiate them from their competitors. These services usually require only occasional attention, but may, in turn, be more profitable than routine work.

Use a message on a clock that reminds the client of these special services—just as Ben Franklin reminded everyone to repair minor problems before they became major catastrophes with his famous: "A stitch in time saves nine"— and trust the message to provoke a comment from the client's client to start a word of mouth conversation. Here are some "timely" messages for clock/watch faces:

AN OFFICE MACHINE REPAIR SHOP COULD USE THE FIRST EXAMPLE, BUT A PR FIRM MIGHT PROVIDE IT AS WELL; A COMPUTER CONSULTANT COULD DISTRIBUTE THE SECOND, BUT ANY SOFTWARE OR HARDWARE SELLER COULD DO THE SAME.

CLIP CALENDARS

*Create preprinted postcards to attach to
an annual calendar.*

Besides the routine and specialized services that many businesses perform for clients, others are involved in tasks that are only of an emergency nature. Take a roofer. While many home owners would inevitably benefit from regular maintenance visits, most call only when there is a leak, lose a shingle, need a gutter repaired, or discover some other problem. The preprinted and stamped postcards, sent by the roofer to his client list, are designed to be clipped to an annual calendar for use of the recipient and for the recipient to send on to a contact, colleague, or client.

The postcard reminds customers as well as friends to schedule a maintenance inspection to prevent future problems. We recommend that roofers—or any other emergency service firm such as plumbers, locksmiths, security companies, and glaziers—provide the maintenance inspections for *free* to form a word of mouth chain that is hard to break.

ROOF NOTES

Our roofer will provide us with our annual free inspection this month to make sure that everything is OK after the winter. He told me that he would be happy to do the same for my friends if they wished to schedule an appointment for him to visit. If you would like to take advantage of this very generous offer, please call Superb Roofing on (848) 368-4095 and tell Bill that you are a friend of mine.

Home Owner

THIS TECHNIQUE COULD BE USED BY HEATING AND AIR CONDITIONING SPECIALISTS, ELECTRICIANS, LANDSCAPE GARDENERS, PAINTERS, AND OTHERS INVOLVED IN EMERGENCY REPAIR WORK.

BATTERY CHECK

*Because batteries often need changing,
create a special reminder for clients.*

Any shop or business that sells any size or type of battery—drug stores, camera stores, grocery stores, toy stores, electronic stores, convenience stores, gas stations, supermarkets, jewelers and the like—ought to send reminders to replace, recharge, check, or rotate the batteries purchased for their watches, clocks, radios, televisions, remote controls, games, flashlights, tools, fire alarms, cordless appliances, calculators, computers, mobile telephones, and other such equipment.

Any battery purchase should trigger a postcard to be completed and addressed by the customer and returned to the store for mailing a prescribed number of months later—depending on the average life expectancy of the battery purchased.

Battery Reminder

If you wish a reminder to replace your recently purchased battery *before* it dies, please fill out the information below, address the reverse side, and return this card to the store.

TYPE OF BATTERY PURCHASED
[AAA, AA, A, B, C, D, N, OTHER]

NUMBER/DATE BATTERIES PURCHASED

INTENDED USE
[RADIO, TOY, FLASHLIGHT, ETC.]

The life of the batteries described above may reach their limit soon. Please come in for replacements as soon as possible and bring this card for a 10% discount on the cost of those batteries.

All Items General Store
1 Shopping Street
Anytown, State

DOCUMENT REVIEW

*Just as batteries need changing,
so professional firms should regularly review
the work they do for clients.*

Lawyers need to be in routine touch with their clients for whom they have prepared wills or estate plans; life insurance agents ought to be in communication with those for whom they have written property and casualty policies; safety and security firms need to talk to those who have acquired an emergency plan from them. Any of these firms should send reminder cards to their clients to reread and revise the appropriate document. Use a double-sided card, inviting the client to check a box or sign a line indicating that the review has been completed. These cards can also solicit approval for the service by asking whether the recipient wants a reminder in the following year.

MANAGEMENT AUDIT

It has been one year since we developed your Compensation Plan. Please review the documents in the Plan to determine whether any amendments or changes are warranted at this time.

Kareful, Akurat, & Barata Consulting

_____
Date

We have reviewed our Compensation Plan dated: _____

☐ The documents are in order now, but would appreciate a reminder notice again next year.
☐ The documents need updating. Please call to schedule an appointment.

_____
Name of Firm

AN UNUSUAL
IDENTIFICATION TAG

Luggage tags are always noticeable while waiting around hotels, restaurants, airports, train stations, bus depots, and taxi stands—and become an easy basis on which to start a conversation with a stranger.

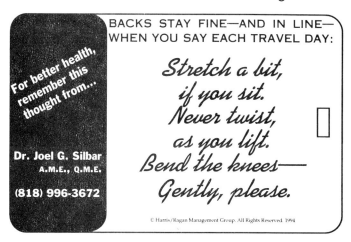

For better health, remember this thought from...

Dr. Joel G. Silbar
A.M.E., Q.M.E.

(818) 996-3672

BACKS STAY FINE—AND IN LINE—
WHEN YOU SAY EACH TRAVEL DAY:

*Stretch a bit,
if you sit.
Never twist,
as you lift.
Bend the knees—
Gently, please.*

© Harris/Ragan Management Group. All Rights Reserved. 1994

The identification tag consists of a message on one side and a name/address card on the other. It is easily attached to suitcases and carryalls with a plastic strap.

We designed the above message for a chiropractor because of the clear relationship to the well-being of his patients. We produced the idea when Dr. Silbar told us that many of the back injuries he treats occurs when patients retrieve their luggage from fast-moving baggage carrousels or out of the back of their cars. The process usually occasions a simultaneous lifting and twisting or reaching motion. The office told us the tags were popular. We hope the message proves to be as well.

VARIATIONS ON THE IDENTIFICATION TAG

We developed tags with slightly different wording and coloring for a number of businesses connected with travel.

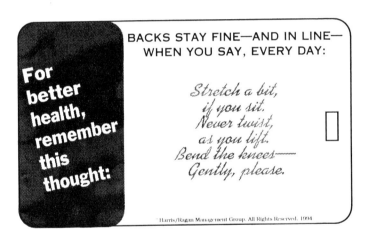

For better health, remember this thought:

BACKS STAY FINE—AND IN LINE—
WHEN YOU SAY, EVERY DAY:

Stretch a bit,
if you sit.
Never twist,
as you lift.
Bend the knees—
Gently, please.

Harris/Ragan Management Group. All Rights Reserved. 1994

We have offered this word of mouth product to dry cleaners, luggage repair shops, locksmiths, service stations, and mechanics—any business, in fact, with a relationship to travel. Why garages? Most people, when they travel, are in their cars and most back injuries seem to occur when people who have been sedentary for a while start hauling their luggage out of the trunk or off of the back seat. Why dry cleaners? Because more often than not it is just before or after a trip that people have their clothes cleaned. The message is a good reminder and does a good deed all at the same time.

THE MOUSE PAD VARIANT

*We suggested this computer accessory with an expanded mnemonic for one of our clients to distribute to **their** customers.*

> **BACKS STAY FINE—AND IN LINE—**
> **WHEN YOU SAY, THROUGHOUT THE DAY:**
>
> *Stretch a bit,*
> *When you sit.*
>
> *Never twist,*
> *As you lift.*
>
> *Draw it tight,*
> *Keep it light.*
>
> *Bend the knees—*
> *Gently, please.*
>
> **PULSATRON TECHNOLOGY LTD**
> **London**
>
> Harris/Ragan Management Group. All Rights Reserved. 1994

Our strategy was that the use of the mouse pad in executive and engineering offices all over the world could spark the kind of conversation that would benefit this English pollution control equipment distributor.

THE SCREEN SAVER VARIANT

Same mnemonic, different design for use with computer screen protection software.

We offered this concept to our computer consultant. His clients now have the option of having this three-part, three-color design sliding diagonally down and across their idle computer screens.

REMEMBER TO SAY,
THROUGHOUT THE DAY:

Stretch a bit,
when you sit.
Never twist,
as you lift.

Draw it tight,
Keep it light.
Move with ease
Gently, please.

THE DUNCAN GROUP
Los Angeles

We suggested that the item be sent to clients on 3.5" disks with appropriate instructions for installation.

BECAUSE OF POTENTIAL COMPATIBILITY PROBLEMS, CRAIG DUNCAN OF THE DUNCAN GROUP ONLY SUGGESTS OFFERING AN INDIVIDUALIZED SCREEN SAVER MESSAGE THAT CAN BE INSERTED INTO A COMMERCIALLY AVAILABLE SCREEN SAVER PROGRAM SUCH AS *AFTER DARK*.

33

DEDICATE SOMETHING TO A CUSTOMER

*Pick a food item in a restaurant, an area in a factory,
or a room in an office suite to name after a customer.*

Every important customer—by virtue of the volume of its business, the longevity of its relationship, the consistency of its orders, or the special help it has provided in the past—is deserving of having an aspect of *your* business named after them—a parking spot, the loading docks, a waiting room, a conference room, even a file drawer.

While restaurants have applied this technique before, we suggest a slightly different approach for them as well as all others. Once a particular dish is named or a suitable plaque erected, invite the customer to be part of an "informal" inaugural ceremony. Feature the ceremony, the plaque, or a photo of the selected facility on a color postcard. Print and stamp the cards for your *customer* to send to its contacts with a message such as the following:

The ABC Company has recently honored our firm by naming their reception area the XYZ Room. *ABC's people have been showing us better ways to do more business with our own customers for years.* *Let us tell you how they have helped us.*	XYZ Company Central Street Major City, ZIP Code State (123) 456-7890

SEE RECIPE NO. 52 FOR THE NAME AND ADDRESS OF A MAJOR POSTCARD MANUFACTURER. NOTE THE INVITATION IN THE LAST SENTENCE OF THE MESSAGE TO TALK TO THE SENDER.

51

CUSTOMER APPRECIATION DAY

*Retail stores should give a bonus discount
to those who bring their friends, relatives,
colleagues, or contacts with them to shop.*

No more than twice a year, select a day or time that features special buys or special prices available *only* to your best customers and *their* friends. Best customers could be those who have recently spent more than $100, those who placed an order that took time to fill, those who have had a charge account in good standing for the past 5 years, or those who have some other distinguishing relationship to your business. Make sure that prime spots in your parking lot are designated for your best customers on Customer Appreciation Day or hire a valet parking service for the occasion.

While sale programs are conducted for special customers by many firms, none that we know about issue the invitation with an *extra* discount for those who bring along a friend. Mail the following card to your customers separately or in one of your regular billing cycles:

> *Please bring this card with you to Customer Appreciation Day. Introduce your guest or guests to a manager, receptionist, or another of our officials. We will overstamp this card with a notation entitling you to an extra 10% above the discount to which all invitees are entitled. Additional cards will then be issued to your guests to entitle them to receive both the special discount and the bonus discount.*

REMEMBER THAT WHEN YOU MAKE IT DIFFERENT, IT AUTOMATICALLY BECOMES REMARKABLE. REMARKABLE EVENTS ARE THE FODDER OF EFFECTIVE WORD OF MOUTH.

GIVE YOUR CUSTOMERS A VALUABLE SERVICE

Provide your moderate income customers for free elements of what you offer your wealthier customers for fees.

Every specialist uses his or her skills in a broad range of tasks. But on close analysis, it is probable that wealthier clients tend to buy an extra level of service or a particular service when compared to that specialist's more moderate income clients.

Once you have isolated the unusual or rare service generally provided for one group over another, begin to offer that service for *free* to the deprived group. It then becomes one of those valuable services that spark conversation and likely a touch of envy among those who would like the service for themselves.

Note that this basic concept has been used in the following Recipes:

- Electricians—No. 36
- Plumbers—No. 37
- Realtors—No. 38
- Dry Cleaners—No. 39.

But also note that these ideas can work, with a change of task and some tweaking, for a number of other retail stores and professional services.

CHRISTMAS LIGHTS

Electricians can offer to erect holiday display lights for their customers.

Some home owners drape a string of Christmas lights over a bush or stretch them along a hedge and others try to nail the lights along a roof line or wrap them around a tree, often with uncertain results. Professional electricians and lighting specialists know how to arrange the same number of lights into a display that causes awe and delight among neighbors and visitors.

Even if the electrician's offer of assistance is confined to making the display safer or more economical, the customer will appreciate the improvements he or she is given and will enjoy the attention drawn to his or her home.

As a result, the customer is likely to recommend the electrician's services to his or her friends, colleagues, and guests—perhaps even to the neighbors as well—in thanks for the extra help received.

WATER FILTERS

*Plumbers can change the drinking water filters
on a periodic basis for their customers.*

Many communities have had problems with their municipal water systems. Even if the water quality in your area has not been called into question, the chemicals in water emerging from a kitchen or bathroom faucet can often be the subject of complaints. While some people have bottled water delivered to their homes—or bring it from a supermarket—a number have now attached special filtration equipment to their faucets. This equipment usually requires the installation of new filters or some other periodic servicing.

It is normally a home owner task, but one that is often forgotten or difficult to do properly. Many would appreciate someone coming around to check and change the filters on a quarterly or semi-annual basis. If homeowners were informed when their plumber planned to be in the area for a *free* home visit to change a filter, many would then identify leaks or other problems that could be fixed at the same time or in the future for the plumber's regular hourly charge.

MOTION SENSORS

*Realtors can arrange to have sensor lights
cleaned and adjusted for their clients.*

Sensor lights are those devices that detect movement within a path defined by an electric beam. When the beam is disturbed, a flood light is automatically illuminated. Over time, the light needs adjustment: Wind, rain, passing trucks, minor earth movements, tree branches, birds, and people disturb the sensitive settings.

At least twice a year, the bulbs and sensing "eye" should be cleaned of dirt and refocused to ensure that the angles are appropriate to offer the intended early alert of someone approaching.

If this service were offered free, once or twice a year, we believe it would spark recommendations and conversations of benefit to the service's sponsor. It is precisely because we know of no one offering this service—and particularly for free—that we suggest it as a valuable, potential word of mouth generator.

WE ALSO BELIEVE THAT CARPENTERS, MASONS, GENERAL CONTRACTORS, PAINTERS, PLASTERERS, AND HANDYMEN COULD ALSO ADOPT THIS SERVICE.

MOTH BALLS

*Dry cleaners can arrange to have
moth balls or cedar blocks checked and replaced.*

Sounds silly doesn't it—someone coming to your home periodically to position moth balls or cedar blocks in your cupboards and closets. But how many people forget to hang moth balls or sandpaper and re-oil cedar blocks to ensure their potency? How many people remember to add fresh moth balls or cedar blocks when adding wool garments to their wardrobes?

Very few, we suspect. Now, what if a local dry cleaner—particularly one anxious to distinguish itself from its competitors—announced to residents in its marketing area that it was offering this service at no charge? Any appointment to place moth balls or cedar blocks could be accompanied with an offer to carry clothes or laundry back to the cleaner's plant for servicing. A postcard requesting the service again could be left with the occupant of the residence at the same time that a service is performed.

Cleaners, of course, need not re-offer the service to those who don't do business with them on a regular basis. People who appreciate the free service and are likely to talk about it to their friends and neighbors are those who will continue to do business with the cleaner on a regular basis. These same people, by the way, can also be asked for referrals to a circle of contacts beyond the individual's friends and neighbors.

DON'T HIDE YOUR MESSAGE

We recommended that the above message be flown over the crowd just before the start of the 1994 Rose Parade in Pasadena, California. The Pasadena political group we were advising at the time wanted to organize a recall campaign against two well-known members of the City Council and were having trouble getting the City's economic establishment to pay attention to the group's funding needs.

While the message may have been a bit mysterious to most of the more than one-half million out-of-town people gathered along the parade route, it drew some notice among the locals; more importantly, it conveyed a big message to its intended audience.

The calls to the head of the political group were so numerous later that day and throughout the ensuing weeks that she eventually selected a representation of the plane and banner as the logo for her group. All in all it proved to be a word of mouth bonanza.

MAKE LIFE EASIER

*Provide potential clients with a
planning document or easy-to-use checklist*

Many service businesses live on word of mouth comments, but find that they work only at a particular point in time. In between, word of mouth comments do little good because the listener does not need the service or product involved. Catering is one of these peculiar businesses. The problem we were given by a caterer was how to generate word of mouth comments long after an event.

We suggested that each host be given copies of an *Event Planning Kit.* The Kit makes it easy for people to prepare for a wedding or party; it has a discreet reminder of the caterer's services and specialities on the back. The idea behind the Kit was to provide something of both value and permanence that could be *given away* by the host or reviewed by a potential client *after* the original event. Here is a sample of one of the forms in the Kit:

Harris/Ragan Management Group 9241 Sunset Blvd., Suite 404 Los Angeles, CA 90069 USA Tel. (310) 278-4018 Fax (310) 271-3649					**EVENT PROGRAM**
		EVENT TITLE			
AT THIS TIME...	**THIS ACTIVITY OCCURS...**	**UNDER THESE CONDITIONS...**	**AT THIS TIME...**	**THIS ACTIVITY OCCURS...**	**UNDER THESE CONDITIONS...**

PHOTOCOPYING PERMITTED   **FORM E**

As something of quality and substance, it was unlikely to be stuffed into a draw, buried in an address file, or otherwise lost in the clutter of everyday life, but saved in a specific place for later reference.

PHOTOGRAPHERS, VIDEO SERVICES, FLORISTS, AND FORMAL RENTAL SHOPS COULD ALSO USE THE EVENT PLANNING KIT. FINE ART AUCTIONEERS COULD USE A SIMILAR CONCEPT IF THE KIT BECAME A PERSONAL INVENTORY RECORD; DRIVING INSTRUCTORS COULD PROVIDE ROAD MAPS FOR THEIR STUDENTS AND THEIR CONTACTS; TICKET BROKERS COULD DO ALBUMS FOR THEATER PROGRAMS, AND SO ON.

WEAR SOMETHING REMARKABLE

*Put on a badge, pin, ribbon, chain, or
some other device that causes others to comment.*

A gentleman we saw cruising the aisles at the London International Book Fair one year was wearing a large gold chain anchored by an enormous enamel and gold oval badge around his neck. He was displaying this obvious mark of an official office over a business suit. We couldn't help but ask about its significance. It was too impressive, too unusual, to ignore.

It turned out that he was President of the Book Publishers Representatives Association in England. He was delighted to tell us about his group, their services, and their relationship to small publishers.

These badges and chains of office, although not uncommon in England, are seldom worn in public; they are generally reserved for official events. The fact that the President chose to wear his badge of office at a trade show was intended to draw attention to the work of the group's members. It clearly worked.

WHILE THIS CONCEPT MAY SEEM SIMILAR TO RECIPE NO. 12, PLEASE NOTE THAT NO. 12 IS FOR CUSTOMERS TO IMPLE-MENT, WHILE THIS RECIPE IS INTENDED TO BE IMPLEMENTED BY SOMEONE IN THE COMPANY.

CUSTOMER AWARD PROGRAM

*Recognize your customers for their help and
award something remarkable to them.*

We have all seen the little gold-toned plastic trophies in novelty stores that proclaim:

They are fun, simulated awards that bring an immediate smile and a lot of lasting pleasure to the recipient. The same idea could be adopted by any business.

Award a badge, pin, banner, trophy, or other similar device—something interesting in terms of shape, color, design, and size—to your customers. Make the award for suggestions, referrals, comments, or recommendations—anything that improves the business or products of the firm. Record the improvement on a framed certificate and present both the device and the certificate at a small luncheon. (See Recipe No. 33 for another way to let potential customers know about such an award.)

RECOGNITION FOR HELP IS ALWAYS APPRECIATED. WE THINK THE DEVICE WILL BE WORN OR DISPLAYED AND IS LIKELY TO GENERATE THE KIND OF QUESTIONS OR COMMENTS THAT WILL ADD NEW BUSINESS FAR BEYOND THE COST IN TIME AND MATERIAL OF A CUSTOM AWARD PROGRAM. FOR ONE COMPANY THAT PROVIDES A WIDE VARIETY OF AWARD CERTIFICATES CONTACT:

Paper Direct
100 Plaza Drive
Secaucus, New Jersey 07094 USA
℞ + (1) 201 271 9609

AN EXOTIC FLOWER DISPLAY

The next time you want to say thank you to a client
for a favor done or a referral made, do it with panache.

A colleague of ours has referred a number of friends and associates to her dentist. To say thank you, the dentist had a huge array of exotic tropical flowers delivered to our colleague's desk—flowers so unusual in color, shape, size, and longevity that people had to stop to comment. Here is a sample of how one of those conversations went:

> *"Who sent you such fascinating flowers?"*
> *"My dentist."*
> *"Your dentist? Why would a dentist send you flowers?"*
> *"Because I'm a great patient."*
> *"No, really, why?"*
> *"I guess because I've referred so many people to her."*
> *"Why would you refer people to a dentist?"*
> *"She really is good, on time, not expensive, and I think others*
> *will like her as well."*

Flowers as a gift or as a thank you are always nice to receive, but seldom evoke the kind of conversation noted here. The difference is that the dentist chose a way to have the flowers make a very pronounced statement.

We think the flowers might have cost as much as $75...expensive in terms of flowers, but inexpensive in terms of any other form of conventional advertising and much more effective, it turns out, than using the same money to give the patient a free cleaning, dinner at a fine restaurant, or a personal gift from a department store. We understand that at least two new people subsequently called the dentist for appointments.

THIS IS A CONCEPT THAT MULTIPLE LEVEL MARKETING GROUPS OR PARTY SALES SPECIALISTS COULD ALSO USE EFFECTIVELY.

EMPOWER YOUR CUSTOMERS

Provide those who buy from you with awards and privileges to share with others—a great way to make new friends for your business.

LET YOUR CLIENTS GIVE AWAY YOUR GIVE-AWAYS

Whenever you decide to give something special away to promote your products or services, let your current clients do the actual giving.

It is natural to want to be the person who makes the presentation of a gift. It is nice to see a reaction of appreciation and it is even nicer to hear that appreciation first hand. But it may not generate as much business as when you let your clients give the item away for you to one of *their* favorite contacts.

In that instance, your clients feel gratitude to you while their contacts feel gratitude toward them. The result is that you keep your clients as strong customers, the clients keep their contacts, and you have the hope of gaining that contact as a new customer in the future.

SEASON TICKETS

*Whether you have permanent seats to baseball,
football, or basketball games or to
philharmonic recitals, rock concerts, or theater groups,
let your customer select the people to enjoy an event.*

Instead of inviting a present customer to a public event, ask your customers to take someone else. Call them to make sure they are willing to participate in your program. Because tickets are time-sensitive and therefore sometimes hard to place, ascertain whether your client will be free on the date of the tickets' availability to accompany their guest or guests to an event.

After the event, it is equally all right to call the customer again, if the customer hasn't called you, to find out who went to the event with them. Ask whether the customer's guest or guests enjoyed themselves and whether any kind of follow-up with them is appropriate from you.

TRY THIS APPROACH. IT IS DIFFERENT. IT IS DESIGNED TO BRING YOUR *POTENTIAL* CUSTOMERS INTO CONVERSATION WITH YOUR CURRENT CUSTOMERS—THE HEART OF THE CONCEPT OF STIMULATED WORD OF MOUTH ADVERTISING. IF IT WORKS AND YOU GAIN A NEW CUSTOMER IN THE PROCESS, YOU WILL FIND YOUR SEASON TICKETS YIELDING MUCH MORE THAN THEY COST.

LOTTERY TICKETS

*Create a drawing for either products you make
or products you acquire.*

In this empowerment variation, the business substitutes lottery tickets for event tickets. The tickets can be purchased from government-run games or from non-profit groups.

In the case of a charity drawing, buy at least two books of tickets—one to give to your customer to keep and one for the customer to give away. Because books of tickets usually consist of five to ten tickets each, you can also ask your customers to share individual tickets among their staff members.

For example, we assisted the Romanian Orthodox Church in Los Angeles with a drawing to raise money to furnish a newly acquired sanctuary. The tickets were $5 each, but books of 5 could be purchased for $20. We bought several books ourselves and gave them away, asking the recipient to pass the individual tickets along to others. All were reminded to fill out the ticket stubs and send them in to be eligible for the drawing.

 Sfinţii Arħangħeli
"ṂIḂAIL şi ḂAVRIIL" Saints Archangels
"ṂICḂAEL & ḂABRIEL" $5
5 Tickets @ $20

Win a $2,000 35" Mitsubishi Stereo Television
with an Advanced Picture-in-Picture Feature
provided by Paul's TV of La Habra
as well as many additional Special Prizes.
Raffle will support the Congregation of the
Saints Archangels "Michael & Gabriel" Romanian Orthodox Church
in its effort to furnish a new sanctuary
for its religious services and educational programs.

MAILING ADDRESS
Romanian Orthodox Church
PO Box 4724
Garden Grove, CA 92642-4724
(714) 530-5350

Date of Drawing: 3:00PM, April 16, 1995
Place of Drawing: At the Church
TV Winner to be notified by telephone

CHURCH LOCATION
4102 Hickman Drive
Torrance, California 90504

ULTIMATE BLACK BOOK

*If you have created a good premium,
developed a proprietary product,
or found an unusual gift, make it available for your
best customers to give away on your behalf.*

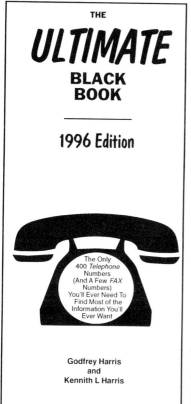

A few years ago, we developed *The Ultimate Black Book*. Its subtitle conveyed everything that needed to be said about the contents of this little reference work: *"The Only 400 Telephone Numbers (And a Few FAX Numbers) You'll Ever Need to Find Most of the Information You'll Ever Want."*

We gave the book to clients of our consulting firm. Soon these clients were asking for additional copies to give to others they knew would appreciate it. We were delighted. It was a way of providing something to our customers that they wanted and something to help our customers further their relationships with their own contacts.

We received several consulting assignments as a result of the impression we made with the book...and the book sold well enough in the open market to justify a second edition.

DOUBLE MESSAGE CARDS

*Create a mailing piece that your
best customers can send to their contacts.*

Word of mouth advertising does, of course, happen by chance, particularly when a film, book, product or event makes such a powerful impression that people talk about it spontaneously.

Most of life's occurences, however, are not so impactful; people sometimes need a little prodding to talk about something with friends, relatives, and associates. Double Message Cards are a good way to get the prodding done.

MESSAGES ABOUT A FREIGHT FORWARDING COMPANY

We developed a Double Message Card mailer for a freight forwarding firm. The mailer consisted of a memo from the company to its customers and two identical, but separable, postcards. The memo reminded customers of the services provided by the firm and offered a discount on the next order placed if they would take the time to address and send the two postcards to their friends, colleagues, or associates. For very good customers—those who had in the past taken the trouble to write to the company to express appreciation—several mailers were provided in the hope that they might send out more than two postcards.

The entire package—printed on 8"x11" card stock—was perforated and folded to become a self-contained mailing piece.

We have reproduced the memo appearing on the left hand side of the opened mailer on the following page; a copy of one of the two identical postcards that each customer of the freight forwarding firm was asked to send is found on page 71.

TO OUR CUSTOMERS:

We have delighted in providing you with packing and shipping services for the past 15 years.

We have also appreciated the consistent support we have received from our satisfied clients.

As a way of saying thank you for your past patronage, we want to give you a
5% discount
on your next shipment with us. (Just send this notice in with your next shipment.)

Please also take a moment to send out the attached discount postcards to those of your friends and associates who you think will appreciate the kind of care and attention we give to every packing and shipping task we are assigned.

If one of your colleagues decides to use our services before the end of 1994, we will give you an
additional 5% discount on all
of your remaining 1994 shipments.

Please call if you have any questions.

Mike Sarbakhsh
Beverly Packing
(213) 658-8365

Dear

We have recently been reminded of the fine service we have received from Beverly Packing of Los Angeles. Our shipments have been tenderly handled, meticulously packed, and promptly dispatched. We have come to believe that they move our goods—from the point of collection to the point of delivery—more efficiently and more carefully than if we were doing the job for ourselves.

If you have a chance to visit their shop on Fairfax at Melrose, you are sure to be dazzled by the variety of goods they ship and the creative packing techniques they employ to get valuable antiques, works of art, cartons of books, and oddly shaped gifts to their various destinations around the world.

We think Beverly Packing deserves to be rewarded for the fine work they have done over the past 15 years. In turn, they have told us that they will give a 5% discount on the first shipment they do for anyone we recommend. This card is our way of referring you to Mike Sarbakhsh at Beverly Packing. If you have any questions, please give me a ring or please just call Mike.

Cordially,

We hoped the recipient of the mailing piece would personally insert the name of his contact at the top next to the word "Dear," sign the card at the bottom, and post it. The address side of the card displayed Beverly Packing's address as well as telephone and fax numbers for the recipient's reference. [Note that the card's actual dimensions have had to be distorted here to accommodate to the book's page size.]

MESSAGES ABOUT A RESORT

The key to these message cards is finding a way to encourage the recipient to take a moment to address the accompanying postcards and send them on.

In the example we designed to promote travel to the U.S. Virgin Islands from Europe through travel agents, we tried to evoke two emotions:

- Fond memories of what may have been a nearly forgotten vacation.

- Generosity in being able to provide a discount for those favored with being sent one of the attached cards.

Do you remember your recent holiday in the United States Virgin Islands?

- Bargain price shopping...
- Thrilling water adventures...
- Your envious tan...
- The variety of enjoyable foods...

Or maybe you simply recall the—

- Lovely accommodations...
- Interesting people...
- Terrific weather...

Perhaps your friends would also delight
in creating their own memories of the
United States Virgin Islands.

If you agree, please take just a moment to address
and post the attached cards inviting them
to review some ideas for a future holiday.

Should your friends decide to visit the USVI,
we will make sure that you are rewarded
for the trouble you took
on *your* next trip abroad with us.

We used illustrations for the Virgin Island postcards. Inserting the name of the recipient's contact and signing the card are in the European tradition; by the same token, no stamp was used because the mailing went throughout Europe and each country's mailing costs are different.

Dear

We were recently reminded of the lovely holiday we had in the United States Virgin Islands. Beautiful weather, lovely sites, interesting things to do—everything we love to talk about when we return from a trip abroad.

The firm that organised our trip wants our friends to enjoy the same kind of holiday in the Caribbean. They say that if you give their office a call (the number is on the reverse), they will send you a brochure and details of a special promotional offer that we can both benefit from.

So if you're starting to consider a holiday of sun, sea, and special sites, the US Virgin Islands might be just perfect. We would be only too pleased to tell you more about what we did, where we went, and what you should be sure not to miss while you are there.

Cordially,

[Note that this double message card was printed on A-10 sized stock. The above postcard measured 15cm x 10.5cm but has had to be distorted here to accommodate to the book's page size.]

POSTCARDS

Retail stores, civic groups, and others should reproduce a photograph, logo, or other symbol on a post card for the use of their customers.

In lieu of a free souvenir, a special postcard can be created to capture the spirit of a particular shopping center, local district, or whole city. The businesses within the portrayed area would be asked to buy these cards with the message side blank. They would then print a small descriptive paragraph on the reverse that links their store's business to the area. For example:

- Come see a museum totally devoted to pets at a 25% discount with this card.
- All taxes and shipping free to anyone presenting this card to All Boots Company.
- Enjoy free beverages with your meal when you show this card to your server.

Once imprinted with the facility's name, address, phone number, and easy to understand directions, leave them around the store, restaurant, or office, pre-stamped with either domestic or foreign postage. Be sure to ask your cashiers and receptionists to offer cards to customers and visitors as they are paying their bills or leaving the facility as a further way to stimulate their use and build future clientele.

To implement this idea, you will need a company specializing in printing full color postcards. For a current price list and sample, contact one of the largest:

US Press
1628A James P. Rodgers Drive
Valdosta, GA 31601 USA
Fx (1) 912 247 4405

CLIENT VOUCHERS

Professionals can create an original certificate—
with a special offer or discount—to give to their best clients
to award in turn to **their** *friends, contacts, and associates.*

A voucher is something of value; when awarded by one client to a potential client, it has more impact than when a professional gives it away on his or her own. For example:

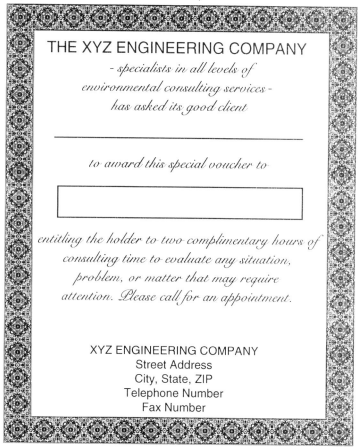

CUSTOMER SPEAK—1

Place a guest book on the counter near the cash register inviting customers to note their favorite employee, aspect of the business, or the best product offered by the establishment.

Not every customer will take the time to write in the book and not everyone who does so will be skillful at recording his or her thoughts. But some gems are bound to be found within its pages.

Once every quarter, review the comments and categorize them, then either:

- Post the results—or any significant points, changes, or trends that may be discerned—for your *employees* to review.

- Print the best comments on the back of pre-stamped post-cards and invite customers to "endorse" the comment by mailing the cards to their friends and colleagues; or

- Conduct a ballot in the store to select the comment that the majority believe best captures the store's ambiance and award a handsome prize to the winning writer.

SEE RECIPE NO. 90, CUSTOMER SPEAK— 2, FOR CONTROLLING THE NEGATIVE SIDE OF WORD OF MOUTH COMMENTS.

CLIENT SPEAK

Invite your customers to "speak" for you with objects rather than words.

Some years ago, the Sheet Metal Workers' International Association celebrated their 100th Anniversary as one of America's most important labor unions. The union leadership chose a metal perpetual calendar as one of the commemorative souvenirs of the event to give to their members and supporters. The calendar was helpful as well as meaningful to the skills of the union's membership.

Our consulting firm had done a number of jobs for the Sheet Metal Workers' Washington headquarters. When we told some of the officials of the union that we were about to make a second business trip to Russia, they suggested giving the calendars to people as a gift. We agreed.

Partially, as a result of this small gesture, the Sheet Metal Workers' International Association are now involved in a project to bring innovative Russian pollution control technology to the United States. Over the next several years, the technology could provide significant work for the union's membership and benefit to the American people. While a great deal of effort has gone into this project, the perpetual calendars played their small part. They offered a chance to explain the potential involvement of the Sheet Metal Workers' International Association, provided credibility to American interest in the Russian technology, and later gave union officials recognition among Russian industrialists.

AD SPECIALITY ITEMS CAN OFTEN "SPEAK" WHEN NOTHING ELSE IS AVAILABLE TO PROMOTE AN ENTERPRISE. AS A RESULT, CHOSE ITEMS CAREFULLY TO REFLECT THE MANY FACETS OF THE MESSAGE YOU WANT CONVEYED. A FEW EXAMPLES CAN BE FOUND ON THE PAGES THAT FOLLOW.

KEY RINGS

Distribute special versions of this ancient necessity.

The idea, again, is not simply for a security company to give away a key ring—something that many companies do at some point or another—but that the key ring selected by the security company "speak" for the security company itself when the ring is given away by someone other than a person associated with the company.

In our mind's eye, such a key ring might include a special tab attached to the ring, each embossed with an individual code number. When a card attached to the ring is mailed back to the security company, information about the keys themselves (their make, type, and traced outline) and the ownership of the ring would be registered. Lost keys might then be duplicated and/or rings returned to the company could be restored to their owners. While duplicating and returning lost keys is a business for some firms, we know of no company that combines these two elements into a *free* service offered by third parties to attract potential clients to the service provider.

THE KEY RING WITH TAB BECOMES A NICE WAY FOR THE SECURITY COMPANY TO GIVE ITS CUSTOMERS A CHANCE TO DO A GOOD TURN AND CREATE NEW FRIENDS FOR THE COMPANY IN THE PROCESS.

OUTDOOR THERMOMETERS
AND RAIN GAUGES

Provide something everybody can use and from which everybody in the subsequent chain of supply can benefit.

The difference between television weather reports of local conditions and reality can be enormous. Television channels cover a substantial area; their reports on precipitation, temperature, and humidity tend to be useful generalizations rather than precise indicators of actual conditions.

Since Americans seem at times consumed by an accuracy fixation—in starting times for the broadcast media, in stock market levels, in statistical measures of athletic performances—businesses can build on that and other cultural markers. For example:

- Fuel oil companies might provide *outdoor thermometers* for their delivery personnel to distribute to customers or for heating and air conditioning contractors and hardware stores to give to their best customers.

- Garden supply firms—whether tool makers, fertilizer manufacturers, seed companies, or the like—might ask each of their retail accounts to distribute *rain gauges* to their customers—one for everyone coming to a nursery before a given date or in response to a newspaper coupon; for those spending more than $10; or in multiples for professional gardeners to give to *their* customers.

LIKE THE KEY RING FOR SECURITY COMPANIES, THE IDEA OF THIS WORD OF MOUTH CONCEPT IS TO LINK NAME AND PRODUCT TO A CHAIN OF RECIPIENTS THAT CAN YIELD BENEFITS THREE AND FOUR LEVELS BELOW THE COMPANY THAT ORIGINATED AND PAID FOR THE IDEA.

PASSPORT TO SERVICES

*Create an eight-page mock passport
offering free services to the holder*

Invite your current clients to take these miniature passports from your office to fill in their names and then give to their friends, colleagues, and associates.

A passport is easy for your local printer to layout for you. Ask him or her to provide blue card stock for the cover and 20# bond paper for the interior 4-page signature, trimmed to a 2 $^1/_8$" x 2 $^3/_4$" size:

[NAME OF CLIENT]	*Passport to Services from the Accounting Firm*
requests that the services described herein be provided to	*of* **KAREFUL, AKURAT, & BARATA**
[NAME OF CLIENT'S CONTACT]	

[DESCRIBE FIRM'S PRINCIPALS, SPECIALTIES, AND/OR HISTORY IN THIS SPACE.]

[PROVIDE THE FIRM'S STREET ADDRESS, MAILING ADDRESS, LOCAL, FREE, AND INTERNATIONAL TELEPHONE NUMBERS, MOBILE PHONE/PAGER NUMBERS, AND FAX NUMBERS HERE.]

2

7

While this is an idea for many different kinds of professional firms and craftspeople—an appraiser's office might offer to calculate square footage at different locations, a physical therapy practice might provide exercise reviews, or a jewelery store might provide free appraisal services—it is also an item that a printing firm might do for free for its professional clients.

When a recipient brings in the "passport" to send a fax or make a photocopy, someone in the firm would write the date and time the service was used and initial the notation in one of the appropriate boxes.

FREE TELEPHONE USE		FREE PARKING	
6			3

FIRST/LAST
PAGES

FREE PHOTOCOPIES		FREE FAXES	
4			5

CENTER
PAGES

59

MINIATURE MENUS

*Restaurants can create a miniature of their menus
to mail on behalf of their patrons.*

Provide your patrons with miniatures of your menu on a fold-over card to create a self-mailer—the front half of the outside cover to be used for the address and postage stamp while the back half can be a photograph or line drawing of the restaurant and/or a map indicating its location. Inside the fold-over, reproduce the entire menu or miniaturize its principal aspects, highlights, or special dishes. At the bottom or along the side, put a message from the chef or owner inviting the recipient to enjoy a complimentary beverage when he or she comes in. Leave the pre-stamped cards on each table, along with pens and self-sticking seals, or provide a few cards and seals at the time the bill is presented.

This concept can be adopted by other businesses substituting samples and/or price lists for the menu and discounts for the offer of wine.

SOMETIMES VERBALIZING POSITIVE IMPRESSIONS IS NOT AS EASY FOR PEOPLE AS WE IMAGINE; PROVIDING THESE CARDS HELPS THEM PASS POSITIVE WORD OF MOUTH MESSAGES TO FRIENDS WITHOUT UTTERING A WORD.

WHAT'S YOUR FAVORITE PART

*Use a postcard to let patrons describe
their favorite aspect of your facility.*

Proprietors often hear a person say: "I love this store!" or "I can always find what I need here." Memorable words to hear. True, but only in part. Nice comments are like the sound of a tree falling in the forest; if no one hears the crash, what impact did the event actually have on others?

Turning nice comments into more than a pleasant complement is not difficult. Place pre-stamped, large format postcards around your facility—in lounges, eating areas, waiting rooms, near cash registers, and at customer service desks. Post little signs near them with some pens inviting people to send them free-of-charge to friends, relatives, or associates in town or elsewhere. To get customers to express their favorite aspect of the store, a message might provide the appropriate lead in:

FGH Store is famous for its motto: "If we don't have it, we'll get it for you." That may be true, but I happen to think that the best thing about this store is...

Put a mock mail box nearby to give realism to the program and some privacy to the comments.

ANY RETAIL STORE, RESTAURANT, OR OTHER FACILITY SERVING THE GENERAL PUBLIC CAN USE THIS CONCEPT. SEE RECIPE NO. 52 FOR

THE ADDRESS OF A CUSTOM CARD MAKER.

A VOUCHER SYSTEM FOR PROFESSIONALS

Develop a voucher that entitles the holder to a particular service.

Once you have decided on the particular service that you are willing to provide to prospective clients for free, at a discount, or for no charge if performed in conjunction with some other service, print the information on a card for your current clients to give to *their* contacts.

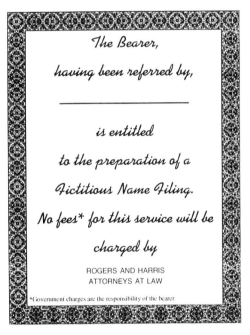

IN LIEU OF A FICTITIOUS NAME FILING LAWYERS COULD OFFER TO REVIEW A WILL, LOOK AT A CONTRACT, OR RESPOND TO A SUMMONS; CONSULTANTS COULD OFFER TO WRITE A LETTER TO PUBLIC AUTHORITIES, COMPLETE A DEPARTMENT OF COMMERCE OR CENSUS BUREAU SURVEY, OR PROVIDE AN HOUR TO DISCUSS ALTERNATIVE MARKETING STRATEGIES; VETERINARIANS COULD GIVE ADVICE ON HANDLING PETS WHOSE MASTERS HAVE DIED.

A VOUCHER SYSTEM FOR REPAIRERS

Develop a voucher that entitles the holder to a particular service from a professional repair person.

Many customers may enjoy spending social time with their contractors, plumbers, or mechanics, but dislike dealing with them on a professional level. No matter how friendly and helpful someone in the repair field can be, people generally only see them when something of value is damaged or broken. Whatever the reason for a visit, it is generally associated with extra cost, unpleasant pain, or time-consuming bother.

The voucher below is designed to be given out to existing clients for transfer to as many of their contacts as possible and to answer one of the common concerns of anyone faced with the necessity of a visit to a repair facility.

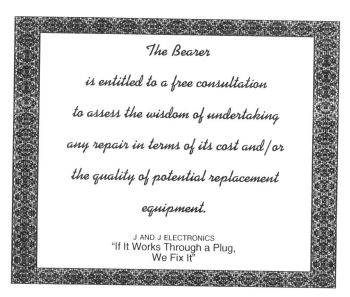

The Bearer

is entitled to a free consultation

to assess the wisdom of undertaking

any repair in terms of its cost and/or

the quality of potential replacement

equipment.

J AND J ELECTRONICS
"If It Works Through a Plug,
We Fix It"

FAVORITE SAYINGS

*Identify your business or activity with
a saying, slogan, or theme and put it everywhere.*

Ben Franklin wrote *Poor Richard's Almanac* and filled it with timely and meaningful thoughts, some of which still motivate us today. We have already mentioned his justly famous: "A stitch in time saves nine." There were others: "Early to bed and early to rise, makes a man healthy, wealthy, and wise" and "God helps them that help themselves." Some people, of course, are motivated by more modern thoughts: "When the Going Gets Tough, the Tough Get Going" or "Just Say No!"

Each of us has a favorite theme or saying that motivates or defines our goals and/or reflects our approach to business. Capture it on a shirt, hat, scarf, the wall plaque, decal, refrigerator magnet, pennant, bumper sticker, or any other common display device and give it to your customers—along with your name, phone number, and identifying logo to pass along to others. Here is our favorite of the moment

GET IT RIGHT

Harris/Ragan Management Group • (800) 966 7716

PROVIDE INFORMATION AND THEY'LL SEND OTHERS

Give your customers new, important, or humorous information to share with others and benefit from the ensuing discussions arising from the inevitable: "Where did you hear that?"

THE REMINDER STICKER

*Print self-stick labels for your client's use
with important information for them on it.*

It is the bane of business life today that phone books and Rolodex files encourage alphabetical listings while most business people think in terms of subjects or products. They know they need the plumber, but can never remember whether the name of the firm is "R_X For Plumbing," "Plumb Medics," or "The Plumbing Doctor;" they know they want to speak to Greg or Kirt, but never know the guy's last name because these never seem to get sewn on a work shirt.

We have a better solution than hoping customers will look you up again in the Yellow Pages or ask someone else. We suggest giving customers informational stickers to post as reminders. For example:

- The best sequence for providing key information to 911 Operators for all telephone cradles;
- *"Lights Off"* stickers for rooms, closets, hallways, and other places where lights tend to be left on;
- *"Save Your Data"* stickers for the frame of your computer screen or the face of your copy easel.

Be sure that whatever sticker you provide your customers that each carries the name of your firm and your telephone number.

The closer the relationship between the permanent message and the business of the company the better. We would put a sheet of these stickers in with each invoice for new customers and send them at least once a year to old customers. And, of course, we send a sheet or two extra along with a Post-It note asking the customer to pass them along to friends, relatives, and associates.

BUSINESS TOURS

Encourage teachers at your local schools to bring their students for a tour of your facility.

Making the process of putting products in stores or providing complex services to customers real to young students is a challenge. Moreover, teachers appreciate opportunities to show how work done in the classroom relates to work done on the job.

While business tours are certainly not new, targeting children and young people as your tour audience may be. Rather than aim at potential customers, you are aiming at future ones and their relatives. Children are great vacuums—sucking up information as it comes to them to be reprocessed at other times in other contexts. They are also wonderful megaphones capable of broadcasting what they heard and saw to others.

Tours can be periodic as well as regular; they should be well thought through to provide information in an orderly and interesting manner. Provide a souvenir—a pen, pencil, or other personalized item—at the conclusion of the tour. The recipient is bound to show a parent, grandparent, uncle, cousin, or friend what he or she received...and the ensuing talk about what the young person saw or learned from the tour may result in both new business and good will that will more than compensate for the cost of the program.

IT'S THE SEASON FOR CHANGE

*Send a regular reminder—annually or every six months—
to clients to do things for themselves.*

Sometimes word of mouth stimulation can be gentle; offer a good idea and it will pass from one person's lips to another generally with credit to the business person initiating the idea. It need not be as blatant or as obvious as a coupon, card, or other direct message. For example, you could send postcards with a reminder for clients to:

- Recharge their fire extinguishers,
- Clear their gutters,
- Utilize emergency food supplies,
- Check the tire pressure on all vehicles,
- Plant vegetables,
- Spray for moths,
- Turn sensitive objects away from the sun,
- Spread fertilizer.

or the like. Because of the nature of the reminder, it is probable that recipients will pass the same data along to their own friends and contacts when acting on the advice.

Harry The Handiman

Just a reminder to insert this card behind the light switch plate nearest to your smoke alarm. Remove it when you...

TEST THE SMOKE ALARM BATTERY!

(200) 555-1212

PRODUCT UP-DATE

Computer software companies have mastered the upgrade reminder, creating a captured market in the process for every change in their products.

Other businesses can use the same technique to let old customers know that new ideas, designs, or technological advances are available that will make their equipment work better, their processes flow more smoothly, or their lives feel easier. Hardware stores can talk about new hand tools; garages about new diagnostic equipment, and adjusters about new measuring devices.

In each case, as with all the other word of mouth reminder ideas, arm the client with some important idea or information to share with their contacts and colleagues. When the inevitable:

- *"Where did you hear that?"*

or

- *"What a good idea!"*

arises, the word of mouth connection will have been made and the promotional value realized.

THE REMINDER CAN COME TO THE CLIENT IN THE FORM OF A CARD, LETTER, FAX, CATALOG SHEET, BROCHURE, OR ANY OTHER DEVICE WHICH EXPLAINS AND PROMOTES THE IMPORTANCE OF HAVING THE UPDATED TECHNOLOGY.

ALERT-A-MONTH

*Surprise someone with an unexpected
reminder and you may be surprised at the response.*

Whether you remind potential clients by sending them a postcard, running an ad in a local publication, or creating a self-sticking label to attach to a calendar, the technique of reminding someone of something important sparks the type of conversation you want to generate greater business.

The following reminder topics deal with stationery items; it could be sent by anyone at any time. The following month might deal with emergency supplies, then reference books, and so on. Each year the same cycle could be repeated or new items inserted.

Take a Moment to Check Your...

...Business Card Stock   ...Yellow Pads
...Stationery Supplies   ...File Folders
...Toner   ...Mailing Envelopes
...Blank Computer Disks   ...Packing Material
...Cleaning Agents

                       ...other

69

A LEAGUE OF THEIR OWN

Create an organization of related, but non-competitive businesses, to share customers among themselves.

While many business people and professionals recommend specialists in their own *fields* for particular services—a dentist recommends an orthodontist; a dry cleaner recommends a suede specialist; an entertainment lawyer suggests a bankruptcy lawyer—few move outside of their own professional fields.

We suggest working hard to create a league among service businesses in a particular geographical area. Formalize the league by giving it a name, collecting dues, printing informational booklets about the members and their specialities, and providing a special free gift to new customers sent by other members. Establish common policies of services, hours, returns, discounts, sales, and more.

We implement this concept informally at book shows we attend on behalf of one of our affiliates, International Publishers Alliance. When a visitor to our stand asks us a question outside of the interests of our participants—a recommendation for a specialty publisher, say, or a printer, distributor, agent, or other specialist—we always hand them a card with our written recommendation to carry to another person at another stand at the show. The visitor likes it because he or she will then appear at the new site with credentials and the company recommended is flattered that new potential business was sent its way.

FOR A RELATED WAY TO GENERATE BUSI-NESS FOR AN AFFILIATED GROUP OF STORES OR OFFICES, SEE RECIPE NO. 24

PUT YOUR BEST AND YOUR BRIGHTEST OUT FRONT

Select and reward your most enthusiastic and capable employees to be first to respond to customer needs.

In only a few areas of human endeavor, decision makers are purposefully put on the front lines to work—when piloting a plane, arguing a case in court, or doing triage in emergency medical situations, for example. In most areas, however, the lowest ranking, least experienced persons usually find themselves on the front lines dealing with sometimes hostile, often confused people. While the receptionists, telephone operators, clerks, and soldiers are up front, the bosses and knowledgeable employees are usually at the back doing other work.

But putting some of your best people up front, even if only on a rotational basis for a day or two a month, provides a dose of reality that is hard to get elsewhere. It also might change the attitudes of potential customers about the entire organization when they receive fast, thoughtful, and thoroughly competent responses to both trivial and difficult inquiries from the first person they talk to.

That kind of reaction might generate word of mouth comments faster than more cash registers or lower prices.

ANSWERING BASIC QUESTIONS

Train all employees—from the lowest to the loftiest—how to respond to key questions about your business.

Those who are often in closest contact with customers—particularly in the hospitality industry—are often the least able to communicate with them. The porters, maids, gardeners, drivers, guards, and repair personnel are seldom trained in the basic philosophy, goals, and mechanisms of the company they work for. Simple questions that should be answered quickly, often only confuse them.

In contrast, think of the receptionists who work in Russian office buildings; they personally guide individuals inquiring about a firm to the proper office. Think of the chief petty officer at the gangway of a ship who escorts personnel to their destination on the appropriate deck. Think of the hosts at ski resorts who not only respond to questions, but willingly take a run with vacationers to show them various routes.

The first group of employees tend to generate some frustration, a slight annoyance, a touch of impatience among customers—attitudes that customers will carry away from a hotel, restaurant, or entertainment complex and use when describing any of these facilities to friends and relatives. The second group of employees generate the opposite feeling in customers—feelings of warmth, comfort, and caring. Those kinds of feelings are sufficient to get even the most taciturn individual to be effusive about a place visited.

THIS CONCEPT IS BASED ON THE PRINCIPLE THAT THE CLOSER AN EMPLOYEE IS TO THE CUSTOMER, THE MORE RESPONSIBILITY THE EMPLOYEE HAS FOR THE WELL-BEING OF THE BUSINESS.

ANSWERING BASIC QUESTIONS—
IN ENGLISH

Many employees who are in closest contact with customers don't speak English!

Speaking a language that is not your native tongue is more a function of exposure, than education. We often forget how facile children of three and four can sound when we hear them speak in a foreign country, often leaving us dumb-struck by their prattling in a language that we may have struggled to learn after years of study.

Realizing this suggests that those with a weak command of English can be taught pronunciation skills, a basic response vocabulary, and key phrases in a short period of time. The U.S. Army devotes about 10 hours to this kind of rudimentary language training for new transfers to units in Germany. We recommend that you ask a local language instructor or firm to construct a 10-to-20-hour course—divided into one or two hour periods—in which at least a portion of the time is spent on questions commonly asked by customers in a variety of simulated accents.

A less expensive, but effective way, to proceed may also be to buy a tape course from professionals expert in helping people lessen their regional and/or foreign accents. For information on one very good series of audio tape courses available, write:

ZWL Publishing, Inc.
PO Box 7991
Dallas, TX 75209-8255 USA
℞ (1) 214 350 0273

CUSTOMER RESPONSE MANUAL

*Prepare a manual with the
most commonly asked questions
and the most current answers.*

Questions still arise and responses still need to be provided, even for your new native English-speaking personnel, even when your best employees cannot be up-front, and even while your newest employees are trying to master English.

We believe that one way to solve the problem is with a clearly divided, well-indexed manual containing the most commonly asked questions and the best answers. These not only help less knowledgeable employees respond to customers, but lets customers themselves solve their own needs by reviewing the book.

We recommend putting each question and its answer on separate page of the manual, to allow for expansion and/or changes as required.

THE CUSTOMER NEWSLETTER

*Share not only news of your special offers and
new acquisitions, but inside news of your industry as well.*

Most newsletters aimed at customers are either barely disguised advertising circulars or employee-of-the-month bulletins. Generally, very little of substantive interest to the customer can be found in them.

We believe that these journals ought to be used to discuss how elements of the industry—news items usually found only in trade papers—may be affecting your company. For example, if printers talked about anticipated paper shortages with their customers—due to environmental limitations on tree cutting, excessive demand in another area, or any one of a hundred other factors—customers would be more understanding of subsequent price rises and better prepared to conduct their own business. They wouldn't resent the printer's price rises or the broker's increasing quotations, but work a little harder to deal with the new situation on their own.

Inside information is hard for outsiders to get. Customers regularly supplied with this kind of information are likely to show their appreciation in the process. Because the source of such information is often volunteered to a third party or sought by them, the basis of a meaningful word of mouth conversation is laid at almost no cost.

75

KEEP IN TOUCH

*If formal newsletters seem beyond your capabilities,
send Good News/Bad News Notes from time to time*

Staying in touch with customers who need you only when they need you—but not often, perhaps, and not regularly—is difficult. Finding a way to keep your name and service before these customers is challenging.

One professional told us he changed his offices every two or three years just so he had an excuse to send old customers and new prospects an announcement card as a reminder that he was still available for their business. We found this a bit extreme as a way to catch people's attention and remind them of his services, specialties, and interests.

Instead of this, we recommend sending a fold-over card with a news note about your industry—some new technical development, government regulation, economic event, or odd statistic. If your type of business has been the subject of some cartoon, borrow the basic theme or alter a name to get the same impact as the original. Mail the cards on a regular basis to your customers and you won't have long to wait for long lost clients to call or new referrals to appear.

LIMOUSINE SERVICES, LOCKSMITHS, CABINET MAKERS, AND OTHERS NEED WAYS TO STAY IN TOUCH. SEE RECIPE NO. 2 AND RECIPE NO. 41 FOR RELATED IDEAS.

WHATEVER STICKS TO THE CEILING

Offer your posters and other large format advertising for the ceilings of rooms where people rest.

Blood banks, rest homes, hospital rooms, trauma center halls, emergency shelters, and other facilities have people who spend a lot of time on their backs staring at blank ceilings. Give them something pleasant to *think* about while providing visitors and employees of these facilities with something worthwhile to *talk* about.

All in all, the concept of decorating ceilings becomes a nice way to recycle items that might otherwise be thrown away and helps generate word of mouth conversations among those who may be able to act on the product or destination illustrated on the posters in the future.

TAKE CUSTOMERS INTO
YOUR CONFIDENCE

*Letting customers know about both the
positive and negative aspects of your business
can build loyalty and generate support.*

Feeling like "one of the family" in a family business means that you enjoy the benefits and suffer the disappointments of other members of the family.

When nearly all aspects of your business—price, quality, terms, and convenience—are fairly equal between you and your competitors, this concept of sharing may be the key to your growth.

Customers who are made to feel like one of the family are more loyal and the loyalty can translate into speaking vocally about you, your products, and services to others.

KEEP 'EM LAUGHING

Pass good jokes along to your customers and
their *contacts are likely to ask:*
"Where'd you hear that?"

Businesses that exhibit a sense of humor are always talked about, especially when the joke's on them. Some of the best of these appear in widely-seen advertisements in magazines and on television and generally evoke considerable comment.

Small business people can generate the same level of appreciation when jokes relevant to their industry are regularly passed along to their customers. We favor a chain letter approach where a joke is printed on 3"x5" cards or half-sized stationery with a brief notation such as the following:

> PASS THIS ALONG TO AS MANY PEOPLE AS POSSIBLE
> TO PROVIDE AS MANY SMILES AS POSSIBLE.
>
>
> XYZ ASSOCIATES
> Major Street
> Anytown, State

Once received by the recipient, the joke is likely to be repeated to friends, colleagues and associates by telephone, fax, E-Mail, or copied and re-mailed in the regular post.

79

LET ME STUDY THAT...

*Getting people to talk about the
untalkable sometimes requires a "study."*

Who does your remote microfilming for you is not usually the stuff of ordinary conversation among casualty lawyers, claims specialists at insurance companies, or officials of government agencies. So to create a little word of mouth on behalf of our client, American Microfilm Company, we suggested the firm offer to analyze a prospect's remote copying costs.

We knew that while many firms in the records copying field tend to ask for a similar per page copying and reproduction fee, there are wide variations in what they charge for multiple copies, mileage covered, time spent, process services, legal filings, minimums, and so on.

We felt that in studying what a business pays for its services, our client would have a double advantage: The firm could refine its own pricing policies to be more competitive while at the same time offering a valuable service for free. In the end, the recipient of the study would learn more about his or her own business and might end up with long term cost savings in the process. That, we reasoned, becomes the stuff of conversations that generate new business.

NEVER HIDE YOUR LIGHT UNDER A BUSHEL

Let your customers know exactly—and often— why your business is different from its competitors.

One of the impressive techniques of astute marketing people has been to lavish fancy adjectives or an expansive description on a new product. They were known as "Famous Amos" cookies long before they, in fact, became renowned; it was called "Paul Bhalla's Fine Indian Cuisine" well before any outside restaurant critic confirmed the description; it is often the season's "most talked about (or most controversial) film" weeks before enough people have actually seen it to comment sufficiently to warrant the description.

The principle is worthwhile. People sometimes need a boost to feel good about being the first to try a cookie, restaurant, or movie. So it is with new customers acquiring established products for the first time; they often need help in explaining why they tried something new or different; why they switched from some old standby. Help them! Give them some reasons that makes a business, service, or individual product stand out from all other similar products. If nothing else, start by trying to fit one of these standard descriptors to your product:

- Least expensive
- Highest volume
- Oldest
- Proven
- Newest

PAY ATTENTION TO REACTIONS AROUND YOU

How people deal with each and every aspect of your business yields important clues about what they will say about your business and products to others.

EAVESDROPPING IS NOT ALWAYS IMPOLITE

Find places to listen to your customers talk and learn how you can improve your business.

It often happens that people are too busy to reveal their true feelings or too shy to talk about them in front of strangers. Others have been carefully taught that if you don't have anything nice to say to someone, don't say anything at all. Very understandable, but not very helpful to a business seeking to improve itself and build on positive word of mouth advertising.

As a result, focus groups, questionnaires, and other *formal* ways to ascertain people's impressions do not always provide valid data. Honest feelings can remain suppressed in these forums. Because of this, eavesdropping may be a very good source of information about your business. Front doors, parking lots, elevator lobbies, food courts, exhibit stands, lounges, and information centers are all useful places where people gather and often articulate their expectations, confusion, or impatience with some aspect of your business.

Position yourself—or members of your staff—in any of these places from time to time to listen to your customers.

WATCH 'EM READ

Observing exactly how people react to the written word often reveals volumes about their true feelings.

We have made the point before that not all word of mouth comments are expressed verbally; some arise from body language, facial expressions, and physical interactions. As Roy Disney once noted about show business: "When heads are still and seats aren't squeaking, you know its working."

We once sold items regularly at swap meets. It didn't take long to realize that those who looked at the merchandise while their bodies were at a 90° angle were hardly ever buyers; those who physically turned to face the display often were. We soon learned to pay more attention to body movements than to other clues—such as dress, jewelry, and language to estimate spending power and interest.

Watching people confront an advertisement, directional aid, poster, pamphlet, book, or other document can offer important clues about the clarity of the material and the impact of the presentation. When you are observing reactions, never hesitate to ask why their eye movements stopped, why they frowned, why they may have looked puzzled, or why they smiled, nodded, shuffled, stared, or otherwise reacted to what they were reading.

These observations will help you improve your material immeasurably in the future and give you an indication of what will be ignored and what will be talked about.

FIRST IMPRESSIONS CAN BE AMONG THE STRONGEST

Capture your customer's initial observations to reinforce the positives and corrective the negatives they perceive.

First impressions are not only strong, they are often quite different from subsequent observations. First impressions usually deal with the physical attributes and visible aspects of a situation; later, when people become more familiar with their surroundings, more subtle nuances of interpreting information and determining relationships emerge. As a result, it is important to learn about first impressions before substantive concerns intervene to alter those original perceptions.

To capture first impressions, interview new employees in the week they start working. In addition, retailers might station someone from time to time near the principal exits to ask people whether they had just completed their first visit to the store. Those who respond affirmatively should be asked whether they would like a substantial gift certificate in return for consenting to be interviewed then and there about their first impressions. Those who agree to be interviewed should be asked a series of questions around the following topics:

- *The purpose of their visit.*
- *How easy it was to accomplish their mission.*
- *What directional signs did they look for?*
- *Did anything in the store surprise them or annoy them?*
- *If they were to recommend shopping at this store, what might be some of the things they noticed that might be worth mentioning to a friend?*
- *What would they do differently on their next visit?*

COMPUTER LITERACY

Create a special file on your computer reserved for the profiles of your customer's likes and dislikes.

Intelligence services around the world live by the maxim that all information is valuable, but not necessarily immediately usable to achieve a particular goal. Collecting and evaluating information is often tedious, but usually rewarding.

Most businesses do not gather useful information on their customers in any central place, relying on statistical generalizations compiled by others or the institutional memory of the boss, a secretary, or a receptionist to remember important details. Most businesses do not see their customers on a daily or even weekly basis; while contact may be frequent and intense over a relatively short period of time— a lawyer preparing a client for testimony in court; a small publisher working with a designer on a cover; a special occasion restaurant planning a birthday party; an architect designing an extension to a room; a restorer repairing a broken vase—most of the time months may pass between meetings.

Yet nothing makes a stronger impression than being able to remember the details of past activity with a customer and being able to confirm vital information to make any new project move forward more expeditiously.

We think all businesses should try to develop customer profiles. As an example of what might be captured in this data base, here is what a *restaurant* might record beyond the obvious name, address, and telephone numbers (home and office):

- Menu choices—appetizers, main courses, desserts, beverages—for both host and guests.

- Table preference—inside, outside; booth, window, smoking/nonsmoking.
  + Server preference, if any—by name or by attitude (attentive? passive?).
  + Atmospherics—quiet privacy, visible spot to others.
  + Method of payment—cash, check, credit card (American Express, Diner's, Carte Blanche, Discover, Visa, MasterCard, other).
  + Celebratory dates—birthday, anniversary, holiday, special occasion (Secretary's Day, Valentine's Day, contract award).
  + Day and dates of previous visits to establish a pattern.

Look how this kind of information, printed out for the restaurant's host to review before seating the customer on his or her next visit, might yield in the way of pleasure:

"Nice to see you again, Mr. Thornton. May I get Ella, your server again this evening, to bring you the usual iced tea? Wonderful. Mrs. Thornton: A Coke, no ice?

"I recall how fond you are of our salads. Besides the Cobb you had the last time you with us, we now have a new Mexican-style salad and a Ceasar on the menu. I remember also that you remarked on our breads. If memory serves me, we even brought your party a couple of refill baskets. In any case, we have some new selections this month—a French roll and a Russian black bread—that I think you will enjoy. Let me know instantly if you need anything redone or refilled to make your meal more enjoyable."

If you were Mr. Thornton, making a return visit to this restaurant after perhaps a six month absence, would you be impressed? Do you think you or your guest might talk about the level of service and attention at this restaurant? We do. We also think this kind of attentiveness is the basis for important word of mouth advertising.

THANK YOU'S THAT PACK
A POWERFUL PUNCH

When clients chance to tell you about why they keep coming back, why not give them a way to tell others the same thing?

Some businesses have a pleasant ritual of sending thank you notes to customers at the conclusion of any given task. While they are nice to receive, we have often wondered whether they add anything to getting new jobs from the same client—or the client's contacts.

We believe that those business people who are inclined to send such cards are probably already recognized by the client as thoughtful, caring, and appreciative. Thank you cards probably add little to the impression. Instead, we suggest sending a little certificate which allows the satisfied customer to convey to others the very qualities that a thank you card can only imply:

XYZ ASSOCIATES
*in appreciation for the work
recently concluded for*

[INSERT CLIENT'S NAME]

*invites the principal's of the firm
to send this card
to another company
that might have tasks that would
help them
accomplish their goals.*

We would also suggest that a cover letter be sent with the certificate to the customer:

Date   **XYZ ASSOCIATES**
                                    Main Street
                                  Major City, State

Dear Mr.Prince:

We thoroughly enjoyed the time we
spent on your project and delight
in the fact that the end result
turned out positively for you.

We have enclosed a certificate that
you may be able to pass along to a
colleague or contact. In appreciation for the work done and for your
help in our growth, we will provide
a 10% discount to anyone you refer
to us and a 15% discount on all
future work for you.

                    Sincerely,

                    X. Yale Zanville
                    President

THAT'S A PRINT

Publish the suggestions and ideas that customers provide you in a book.

Some of our clients are very bright, articulate, and outgoing—the ones who tend to call talk radio programs, submit letters to the newspapers, or organize events to support good causes or protest bad projects. These same clients are also likely to put their thoughts about a business—both positive and negative—in writing.

Encourage it. Ask people to jot down their ideas and send them to you; tell them that you want to show the creativity of your clients and you are planning to publish a book of their thoughts called: *"We Listen."* Each contributor will receive 5 copies of the finished book— one for themselves and several to give away. Then, reproduce all or parts of the best letters received within a specified period with a comment from you on how the idea was used or why specifically it could not be incorporated.

For assistance in producing a book, see the advertisements in any recent edition of the *PMA Newsletter* for the names of professional editors, writers, designers, illustrators, typographers, printers, and other specialists catering to publishers. Write for a copy of a recent issue of the newsletter to:

Publishers Marketing Association
2401 Pacific Coast Highway—Suite 102
Hermosa Beach, CA 90254 USA

THE CONTEST

Encourage a local middle school
to organize a writing contest around the theme:
"Why I Would Like to Run a Business Like XYZ Associates"

Nearly all kids get asked, at some point during their growing up years, what they want to do when they have to earn a living. The answers often become the stuff of family legends—either because they evoke a smile for their off-the-wall nature or because they reflect some intense current interest that may fade over time.

But posing the question in terms of a local business offers a fresh way to help focus them on the nature of various jobs and helps make their continuing education seem more relevant. It also helps the contestants and their relatives come to appreciate the target business better.

The rules of the writing contest should include a requirement to interview the owner, employees, and customers of the sponsoring business; to list why the exciting aspects of the business are attractive and why even the routine matters can be interesting; and to review newspaper articles and/or other literature about the place of the business's industry in the national economy. The sponsoring business should provide a substantial prize and publish the entries in a booklet for each student to take home so that others come to understand your business as well.

ALTHOUGH THIS IDEA FOCUSES ON A SMALL WORD OF MOUTH TARGET—THE CHILDREN'S EXTENDED FAMILY—IT CAN HAVE A FAR REACHING IMPACT OVER THE YEARS.

RUN INFORMAL FOCUS GROUPS

*Conduct discussions from time to time among
small representative samples of your customer base.*

Focus groups are often used to gauge reaction to a business or product. Because they permit in-depth questioning, they yield information that yes/no surveys cannot provide.

Say you want to improve your customer services. Here are the type of questions you might pose to a group of six or eight customers seated comfortably around a conference table or in a private room at a hotel:

- *What do you expect or want to hear when you order a product on the telephone?*
- *Is knowing your purchasing history—type, quantity, price, credit preferences, payment choices—meaningful in dealing with this business?*
- *Is confidentiality about your name, address, and purchasing history important to you?*
- *What do you admire most about businesses that treat their customers well—their exchange policies? their on-time reputation? their delivery services? their well-staffed departments?*

Be sure to reward your panelists for their time. Also keep in touch with them as progress is made in implementing the suggestions emanating from the focus group. They, themselves, can become an important source of word of mouth commentary about the company or the product by virtue of their involvement in the project.

MINIMIZE NEGATIVE COMMENTS

No business can fully avoid negative comments—whether deserved or not—but all businesses can minimize the potential damage through attentive responses to the problems exposed.

MAKE RESTITUTION IMMEDIATELY

*Have a certificate or coupon at the ready
whenever a refund is called for.*

How often have you been to a restaurant, ordered your meal, and then found one or two dishes cold even though the rest are piping hot. Sometimes you can't catch the eye of a server or a manager to complain; sometimes you don't even want to complain for fear of inconveniencing others. Later, when someone comes by to ask the inevitable, "How's everyone doing," the problem may be identified. But it's usually too late to send the cold items back or fix whatever else was wrong. It's never too late, however, to try to make restitution. To do so, immediately offer a free dessert or a coupon for a free appetizer on the next visit to the restaurant.

Please accept a
a free appetizer or dessert
from

Good Food Restaurant

NIPPING NEGATIVE FEELINGS BEFORE THEY CAN FESTER SEEMS TO BE THE BEST WAY TO STOP WORD OF MOUTH COMMENTS THAT CAN TURN DAMAGING. CERTIFICATES AND COUPONS THAT WILL DRAW THE RECIPIENT BACK TO AN ESTABLISHMENT IS A GOOD WAY TO ACCOMPLISH THIS GOAL.

CUSTOMER SPEAK—2

Invite customers to offer constructive ideas
for improving your business

Just as Customer Speak—1 invited customers to identify their favorite aspect of a business or product, so wise business people also invite customers to register their complaints, misfortunes, problems, and suggestions for the same purpose:

To improve the business or a product
and
To generate word of mouth comments.

Moreover, many business people realize that when an individual is invited to get a matter out on the table for resolution, any lingering resentment or nagging doubts about the business or a product can be erased before they can do more serious damage.

These negative expressions should be summarized each quarter and...

- Posted for employees to review; or
- Awarded a prize for the most constructive suggestion.

They should never be ignored.

CUSTOMER SPEAK—1 IS RECIPE NO. 54.

WHAT DOES THE COMPETITION OFFER?

Buy products and services from your principal competitors to study what they do differently from you.

Negative word of mouth comments do not always appear as slam-bang complaints that clearly and forthrightly identify a problem. In fact, most negative word of mouth comments are expressed when something goes wrong and the customer is disappointed. The customer then either announces that no more business will be done with the offending firm or sticks pins in the firm's reputation by sharing nasty comments with friends, relatives, and colleagues.

We have said before that positive word of mouth advertising generally arise when expectations are exceeded and that negative word of mouth comments are usually generated when expectations go unmet. These two thoughts can be expressed by the following formulas:

Level of Expectation + Added Benefits =
Positive Word of Mouth

Level of Expectation - Unfulfilled Benefits =
Negative Word of Mouth

Solving both equations is simple: Learn what the competitors are doing and you will know a great deal about your customer's level of expectation. Determine what added benefits you can provide to *exceed* the customer's expectations and you should generate favorable word of mouth; allowing anything to push the results below the level of expectation and you will likely be dealing with negative comments.

MOCK SITUATIONS

Create questions, problems, and situations to test how your employees respond to complaints, mini-crises, and emergencies.

Every law student is given an opportunity to appear before a mock court—a simulated civil or criminal proceeding where aspects of a pretend trial mimics the real thing. Every soldier participates in war games at a high level of intensity and detail—to understand a little of what a real battle feels like. Every performer takes part in countless rehearsals to be able to simulate reality on stage or film. Every airline pilot spends hours in a simulator to practice responses that may save lives in the event of a real emergency.

It should be no surprise, then, that we believe creating unusual, complex, or difficult situations for employees—when the exercise is safely contained in a classroom or conference room to avoid actual harm or damage—is a useful way for them to learn how to deal with problems whenever they arise.

Mock situations can be generated as simply as asking a friend or acquaintance to buy or return something surreptitiously or they can be elaborately staged events common to local health and safety organizations planning for disasters.

NEGATIVE TIME

*Whenever you ask a customer to do you a favor,
be sure to offer him or her compensation.*

We define negative time as the time spent by someone on projects that offer no foreseeable benefit to that person. Searching a file, locating a cancelled check, reissuing an invoice, repeating an instruction, redoing a report—tasks we all have to do when mistakes are made, details are misunderstood, documents are lost, or problems arise.

Whenever you have to ask people to prove they paid a bill or re-fax a complicated document, be sure to send some kind of gift as a thank you for the trouble they took. It could be a book of humorous sayings, a small tray of dried fruit, or an arrangement of silk flowers; or it could be a discount coupon or courtesy card entitling the holder to some special privilege.

Whatever you choose, be prompt in its delivery and be sincere in your appreciation for the help given. Not only will the gift be certain to stop negative chatter, but it can induce positive comments as well.

GET IT RIGHT

Not only can word of mouth advertising be stimulated, it can be sharpened and directed to produce the results desired.

"ASK ME ABOUT..."

*Making bumper stickers, lapel pins, and
sign boards generate word of mouth comments.*

Slogans such as "I Love Bakersfield" or "I Wish I Were Spelunking" may be pleasing to the city fathers or other active cave explorers, but they do not generate very much word of mouth comment. Making the familiar introductory phrases of "I love..." or "I wish I were...' more specific does indeed stimulate conversation.

Next time, try changing the phrase to:

- *"Check With Me Why I Love Bakersfield"*

  or

- *"Be Sure to Ask Me Why I Wish I Were Spelunking."*

REMEMBER TO USE THESE SIMPLE LITTLE INTRODUCTORY PHRASES, WHEN NEXT COMPOSING A PERFECT SLOGAN FOR YOUR BUSINESS, PRODUCT, OR ORGANIZATION. THEY WILL SURELY GENERATE ENOUGH FREE ADVERTISEMENT TO MORE THAN JUSTIFY THE COST OF THIS BOOK.

ASK FOR REFERRALS...DIFFERENTLY

Make sure you know what the customer will say about you before you follow-up on the customer's referral.

Every lawyer learns an important lesson early in his training and career—never elicit testimony in court whose outcome is unknown in advance. Too many lawyers have been surprised, embarrassed, or annoyed by unexpected answers to their questions.

By the same token, when you ask for a referral, be sure to know what the customer will say on your behalf. The easiest way to find out is to ask the customer what he likes about your product or service. Once the customer thinks through what he likes and articulates it, he will sound that much more confident and convincing when the referral listens to the same thing.

The questions asked of the customer, before referrals are requested, should be carefully developed:

- *Does the product/service work for you?*
- *Did you find the price fair?*
- *What aspect of the product or service provides the most benefits to you?*
- *How has the product/service made your work/life easier?*

ANOTHER ASPECT OF THE IDEA OF PRE-PARING SOMEONE TO SPEAK ON YOUR BEHALF CAN ALSO BE FOUND IN RECIPE NO. 9

96

PLAN FOR THE WORST
TO GET THE BEST

*Assume everything that could go wrong will—and
think through possible solutions to each problem envisioned.*

One easy way to plan for the worst in order to achieve the best is to visit a competitor. Become the competitor's customer—or ask one of your staff to play the role of the competitor's customer. Determine what could go wrong in the item you are buying or the process you are discussing with the competitor's staff. Then think through how your business would compare in handling those problems if they were to arise.

One cosmetic company promises to double a purchased product for free (and/or reimburse its cost) if buyers phone an automated 800 number to record their likes or dislikes. The company learns what customers expect and gives customers a way to think through their word of mouth comments.

If you aren't exceeding your competitor's products or procedures, you won't generate much word of mouth advertising. Once you determine what you need to do, make the changes necessary.

TREAT CUSTOMERS BETTER THAN YOU EXPECT TO BE TREATED

*One of the key factors in generating
word of mouth commentary is to exceed the customer's
expectations about the product or service.*

Put yourself in the position of your customers. What do you believe is the basic level of service they expect from your staff or from your product? How does your business stack up against this expectation? Naturally, if you perceive that it is below expectation, you need to bring it up to par. But if you want to generate word of mouth commentary about your business, then you need to exceed that expectation.

What else could you do to make people literally turn their heads or remark to their friends about your business. Make a list. Then determine the cost of each item on the list. Once you have chosen the most cost effective way to exceed expectations, implement the policy to achieve the results you want.

THIS CONCEPT IS APPROACHED FROM A
RELATED ANGLE IN RECIPE NO. 91.

SEEK INFORMATION, NOT APPROVAL

*Ask questions to get information you need,
not questions that yield answers you want to hear.*

Remember the restaurant employee who always asks: "How's everyone doing?" The question is asked in such a way to invariably provoke a "fine" or an affirmative nod. Most people don't want to interrupt their dinners to have a long chat about changing a menu item or a negative conversation that something was cold, or lacked flavor, or was poorly presented. So they take the easy way out; they say nothing.

But if a diner were actually masking what he or she really thought, that person may well express those thoughts to friends and relatives in what could become a negative fashion.

Instead of asking general questions, be more specific. Here are a series of questions that get information restaurants can use to improve their product without forcing their patrons to explain their views or sound negative:

- *Were the potatoes hot enough?*
- *Did you find the vegetables too spicy?*
- *Do you think you made the right choice for your main course this evening?*
- *What can I tell the chef about how you found your meal tonight?*
- *If we could have done one thing differently for you this evening, what would it have been?*

TEST EVERYTHING

Make certain everything about your product or service works better than advertised, but keep that fact quiet.

It is one thing for the owner of a business or product to *proclaim* the advantages of his or her product or service, it is quite another to determine whether ordinary customers can achieve the same results time after time, day in and day out, without any prior experience or special training.

It seems simple enough to suggest continuous testing of products before and after releasing them, but few have the funds to sustain the breadth and variety of tests to anticipate all the problems before they occur and to adjust the product to compensate for these difficulties after they are out. As a result, we urge that testing be as important in your budget as selling, that you make as much effort to test in the after market as you made to bring your product to market originally.

What we have never seen—and think could make the next mega-business success story along the lines of an American Express, Ford, McDonald's, or Microsoft—is a well-tested product that consciously *undersells* what it can really do and let's customers discover for themselves the applications, capabilities, and uses of the product.

Do you think that someone discovering something of value in a product might be excited? Do you think that person might want to share that excitement with colleagues and friends? Do you think the excitement might set off an explosion of word of mouth advertising that might amaze even those who rely on traditional advertising?

START EARLY

*Make every business contact an opportunity
to plant the seeds of a word of mouth comment.*

Sales people are taught that the "close" really begins at the opening of a presentation and actually continues throughout. "You really won't feel safe until you have our fence protecting everything of value to you..." is an example of inserting a closing argument (safety) at the very beginning of a sales pitch for a new fence.

We believe that generating word of mouth advertising can also begin at the outset of a relationship and work for you even if you don't always get the business you seek. One moving company calls itself "Starving Students" and instantly gained business—and conversation—by playing on people's sympathy for what they perceived to be struggling college kids.

Asking for business is the most direct way to stimulate word of mouth comments. Even if the target doesn't need what you are selling, you can still try to stimulate the target's "help" glands from the very beginning. The help glands are located in a mythical part of the conscience where people's desire to do a good deed or be liked or contribute something to someone else are lodged. Also, asking for help directly can dissipate whatever guilt a customer may experience in not being able to buy what you are selling.

Try it. Ask people to help you get business and see how willing they are to pitch in with whatever assistance they can muster.

TELL 'EM WHAT TO SAY

When you are trying to stimulate word of mouth comments, don't leave it up to the customer alone to decide how to promote your business.

Very few things that turn out to be good happen by accident. This also includes word of mouth comments. You have to plant the themes and ideas you want your customers to use when talking about your business. While many do this with slogans and logos, we prefer more subtle mental nourishment.

Remind the customer what it is you do better, faster, cheaper, than anyone in the same business. Give one or two noteworthy examples of what you have done along these lines and for whom.

Try this argument out yourself on the next prospect who calls. If you get a visible or vocal reaction to what you have described, you know you have a winning argument to feed to your customers so they can repeat it to others.

SEE RECIPE NO. 21 FOR A SUGGESTION OF HOW ONE OF OUR CLIENTS PLANTED THE THEMES OF A WORD OF MOUTH COMMENT.

CONCLUSION

You've seen the ads, heard the tapes, and read the copy; they're all over the television, radio, and newspapers in the form of...

- Product testimonials from some expert or other.
- Private conversations between actors captured by herky-jerky hand-held cameras.
- Heavily edited, "spontaneous" post-event interviews with members of the general public.

What makes these examples interesting is that they are all designed to try to *simulate* word of mouth commentary. While imitation may be the sincerest form of flattery, there really is no substitute for the real thing—in word of mouth advertising or in any other field where fakes flourish.

Real word of mouth commentary involves what real people say to each other in private conversations about specific products, services, or events.

To be useful in growing a business or in building sales, word of mouth comments must also be conversations between people who trust each other's tastes, judgments, and attitudes. If it takes only 15 seconds to decide on a dentist—and 15 years to find out if the choice was right—wouldn't you agree that most people feel that talking to friends and colleagues is a better way to choose a dentist than thumbing through the Yellow Pages?

Don't Accept Substitutes

To understand word of mouth advertising better, look at a comparison with other forms of promotion. *Traditional advertising* is when a promoter *buys* newspaper space to urge other businesses to help sponsor a free concert in the park; *public relations* is when other businesses learn about the possibility of helping to sponsor a free concert in the park through a newspaper *article; word of mouth comments* arise when one CEO *tells* another CEO about the advantages of becoming one of the sponsors of a free concert in the park.

While we take nothing away from traditional advertising as a key way to highlight the benefits of a product, service, or event—and nothing from public relations as a useful way to provide additional information about the same products, services, or events—we believe that nothing *sells* quite as effectively as word of mouth.

The Power of Talk

In fact, few have any doubts about its effectiveness. Chemical Bank took a full page ad in *The New York Times Magazine* to proclaim: "...our clients themselves are our single most reliable" means of acquiring new accounts. *Marketer Magazine* reports that food companies rate word of mouth as the "single most important influence on a decision to try a food product." Campbell Soup notes that 90 percent of the public will try something that has been recommended by a friend or relative. A tourism consultant in England states that 70 percent of new business at theme parks comes from positive word of mouth statements while 80 percent of the problems of the industry arise because of negative word of mouth comments.

The impact of negative word of mouth cannot be ignored. Studies conducted by a Washington, DC research firm a few years ago found that only 4 percent of dissatisfied customers provide businesses with feedback on what bothers them, but some 80 percent tell others about their experiences.

Get the Talk Started

Those who have reached this point in the book now realize that word of mouth advertising need not be left to chance. Good luck really has nothing to do with achieving good word of mouth. On the contrary, we hope this book has clearly demonstrated that people will put in a good word about your products, services, or activities if they are a level above their expectations; that to reach this level requires an effort to make what you are already doing a little different to get people to remark about them. And that it only takes a little guidance with the right stimulus to make any product, service or event "remarkable."

ACKNOWLEDGMENTS

William P. Butler   For reviewing and commenting on the text shortly before its publication.

Eve Dutton   For providing administrative assistance and support to keep the two authors linked despite their travels and other activities.

Philip Mudd   For inspiring us—as part of the editorial team at Kogan Page, the British publishers—to undertake this book and to work generally within a format he knew to be popular with readers.

Barbara D. Mayer   For reviewing an early version of the complete manuscript and offering useful and constructive comments for its improvement.

Adolf P. Shvedchikov   For allowing one of us the use of his spacious, airy, and quiet apartment in Moscow where more than 50 percent of this book was drafted.

Tag Powell   For perceptive thoughts on conveying the book's contents through its title and subtitle.

INDEX